TESTIMONIES *by* FAITH

ETHEL M. POLK

authorHOUSE®

AuthorHouse™
1663 Liberty Drive
Bloomington, IN 47403
www.authorhouse.com
Phone: 1 (800) 839-8640

Published by AuthorHouse 04/11/2018

ISBN: 978-1-5246-9266-7 (sc)
ISBN: 978-1-5246-9265-0 (e)

Print information available on the last page.

Any people depicted in stock imagery provided by Getty Images are models, and such images are being used for illustrative purposes only.
Certain stock imagery © Getty Images.

This book is printed on acid-free paper.

Because of the dynamic nature of the Internet, any web addresses or links contained in this book may have changed since publication and may no longer be valid. The views expressed in this work are solely those of the author and do not necessarily reflect the views of the publisher, and the publisher hereby disclaims any responsibility for them.

Scripture taken from the NEW AMERICAN STANDARD BIBLE®, Copyright © 1960, 1962, 1963, 1968, 1971, 1972, 1973, 1975, 1977, 1995 by The Lockman Foundation. Used by permission

I WANT TO FIRST THANK EACH AND
EVERY EDITORS, WRITERS,
PUBLISHERS, PROPHETS OF THE OLD
AND NEW TESTAMENT AND
GONE ON TO MEET THE LORD AS WE
ALL WILL DO, LIKE IT OR NOT,
FOR THE WRITINGS LEFT IN THIS
WORLD TODAY AND DAY BY DAY
SOMEONE IS COMING FORTH WITH A NEW KNOWLEDGE
CONCERNING THE WORD OF GOD.

I CAN NOT CALL NAMES BECAUSE FOR
SURE I WILL FORGET A NAME
AND THEY MAY BECOME DISCOURAGED
NOT CONTINUING THEIR
JOURNEY ON THE ROAD BY FAITH.

MOST OF ALL, COMMENTARIES AND
BIBLE DICTIONARIES ARE GOOD
WHEN YOU DO NOT UNDERSTAND
WORDS THAT YOU COME ACROSS
WHILE YOU ARE STUDYING THE WORD
OF GOD. THEY HAVE BEEN
HELPFUL TO ME AS I HAVE NOW
WRITTEN AND HAD PUBLISHED
TWO BOOKS FROM UNDERSTANDING,
NOT UNDERSTANDING BUT
KEPT STEADFAST AND UNMOVABLE IN
THE WORD OF THE LORD UNTIL
THE DIVINE ANSWER OF INTERPRETATION
CAME THROUGH FROM

GOD BY THE SPIRIT! GOD'S SPIRIT! THAT IS THE SPEAKING IN
UNKNOWN TONGUES AS GOD GIVES
EVIDENCE OF THE TRUTH. THE
TRUTH MAY HURT BUT IT WILL SET YOU FREE!

FROM COMING OUT OF MOM'S WOMB,
I WAS PREDESTINATED AS
ONE OF THE DIVINE ONES THAT
WOULD STAND THE TESTS OF
ENEMIES, DEMONS AND YOU NAME IT.
BAMA, MY GRANDMOTHER
KEPT ME BESIDE HER WHEN I VISITED
AT ALL MEETINGS AT HER
CHURCH. THEY USED TO COME TO
DIFFERENT HOMES AND HAVE
CHURCH. I STILL REMEMBER STANDING
UP SINGING, IT'S ME, IT'S
ME OH LORD, STANDING IN THE NEED OF PRAYER. NOT MY
BROTHER, NOR MY SISTER BUT IT'S ME
OH LORD, STANDING IN THE
NEED OF PRAYER. THE PRAYER OF THE
RIGHTEOUS STICKS WITH YOU
A LOT AND THOSE PRAYERS SURE HAVE DONE JUST THAT.

AT HOME, MOM JOINED CHURCH
AND KEPT ME THERE, ALSO.

WHEN I WILL GROWING UP, BYPU,
SPELLING BEES, BIBLE CONTESTS,
FAMILY PICNICS THAT KEPT YOUR
MIND NOT WANDERING ON
WHERE WAS THE DOPE. STEALING, SELL
YOUR BODY OR GAMBLING.
I AM 68 YEARS OLD BY THAT FAITH
THAT GOD WILL AND CAN DO
ANYTHING BUT FAIL!

I WAS FLYING HOME EVERY TWO YEARS
FROM UP NORTH BURYING
SOMEONE IN MY FAMILY BUT GOD KEPT ME!

HE CAN AND WILL DO THE SAME THING
FOR YOU! JUST TRUST AND
BELIEVE! GET IN THE WORD AND STUDY
BY MANY OF THE BOOKS
THAT I HAVE BROUGHT!

MY THIRD BOOK IS NOW OUT AS I TYPE!

BE BLESSED AND THANK YOU FOR YOUR
PROOF O FAITH THROUGH
YOUR BOOKS!

@ETHELMPOLK

A CONSTANT SMILE

@ETHELMARGARETPOLK

*I CAME FROM A SMALL FAMILY WHO
CARED FOR EACH OTHER WITH
LOTS OF LOVE. WE WERE POOR IN
MONEY BUT HAPPY ON THE
INSIDE. THE FIRST THROUGH FIFTH GRADES, I WAS TAUGHT
BEGINNING LEVELS ON PREPARING
YOUR MIND TOWARD STEPS UP
IN LIFE. MY REPORT CARD WAS
MPTJOMG BUT STRAIGHT A's. I
DIDN'T LIKE NEEDLES. SO, I WOULD
BE FOR REAL SAD AND ABOUT
TO CRY, MOMMA KINDNESS OF LOVE
TOLD THE NURSE NOT NOW
FOR THE VACCINE SHOT. NOT LOT OF
GIRLFRIENDS BECAUSE I WAS
CONSIDERED THE UGLY GIRL IN SCHOOL.
IT DID NOT BOTHER ME
FOR I DID A LOT OF READING, LOOKING
AT EDUCATIONAL MOVIES
AND GAMES SHOWS. I COULD PLAY
THE PIANO BY EAR. IT WAS IN
MY FAMILY OF MUSICIANS. GRANDMOTHER
(BAMA) PLAYED FOR HER
CHURCH.*

*WE DIDN'T HAVE COMPUTERS AS KIDS
IN SCHOOL DURING THAT
TIME. IN ESSENCE THAT WAS GOOD
BECAUSE WE HAD TO LEARN*

HOW TO COUNT USING FLASH CARDS,
YOUR HANDS AND SIMPLE
THINGS TO USE LIKE YOUR FINGERS,
HANDS AND FEET IF YOU HAD
TOO. I WAS MOLESTED IN ELEMENTARY
BY MY TEACHER. HE ASKED
ME TO COME AND GO BACK STAGE AND
HELP HIM SET UP FOR OUR
SCHOOL PLAY. SO, THIS I DID! BEHIND
THE STAGE, HE BEGAN TO
PUT HIS HANDS ON MY BREAST AND
STARTED RUBBING THEM
SAYING, "OH, THEY SO SOFT AND TENDER.
DO THAT FEEL GOOD?" I
WAS SCARED AND DID NOT MORE.
THEN HE SAID, "YOU WILL NOT
TELL YOUR PARENTS, WILL YOU BECAUSE
I KNOW YOU DON'T WANT
TO SEE THEM HURT?" QUICKLY, I SAID,
"YES, SIR AND ALMOST RAN
OUT THE DOOR! MY GRADES FELL
DOWN BECAUSE EVERY TIME I
WOULD SEE HIM IN THE HALL, I WOULD
TENSE UP TRYING TO WALK
BY BUT HE WOULD STOP ME SAYING,
"YOU HAVEN'T TOLD ANYONE
ABOUT OUR LITTLE SECRET, HAVE YOU?"
NO SIR, NO SIR! WOULD BE
MY ANSWER AND QUICKLY WALKED AWAY.

IN JUNIOR HIGH SCHOOL, GUESS WHO
WAS THE PRINCIPAL? RIGHT
HIM, THE MOLESTER! I JUST COULD NOT
STUDY FOR THE THAT SICK
SMILE ON HIS FACE!

I JOINED THE BAND AND PLAYED THE
CLARINET. WE TOOK LOTS OF
TRIPS WINNING NUMBERS OF CONTESTS WITH TROPHIES.
SCHOLARSHIPS WERE OFFERED AFTER
GRADUATION BUT I MET A
BOY IN SCHOOL AND GOT PREGNANT
AFTER THE FIRST TIME HAVING
WHAT YOU CALL SEX. AFTER I HAD MY
CHILD, I GOT MY GED FOR
HIGH SCHOOL. THEY WERE TOUGH
THEN. YOU WENT TO SCHOOL
LIKE ORDINARY SCHOOL WITH TOUGH TEACHERS.

MY PARENT NEVER MARRIED BUT SET
GOOD ROLE MODELS FOR ME
AS I GREW UP. DAD NEVER HIT MOM
NOR DID I SEE THEM FIGHT.
WHEN I MARRIED, WRONG! IT ENDED
IN DIVORCE BECAUSE OF NON
COMMUNICATION TO SOLVE ISSUES.

NEVERTHELESS, I AM SOLVING HORRIBLE
ISSUES IN HIS LIFE AND
FOUND OUT BE WERE NOT ACTUALLY
DIVORCED. THE STORY GOES
ON! LOOK FOR MORE PUBLISHED BOOKS
AND A POSSIBLE MOVIE!

I WOULDN'T DO NOTHING ELSE BUT
SMILE BECAUSE GOD! GOD HELD
MY HAND AND HE HAVE KEPT ME THIS
FAR! I STILL FIND NO FAULT

AND WILL CONTINUE TO WALK, RIDE
OR CRAWL DONE THROUGH
MY VALLEY OF THE SHADOW OF DEATH!

BE BLESSED!

@ETHELMARGARETPOLK

MY DREAM

AS I GREW UP AND KEPT THE FAITH, THE THOUGHT OF PEOPLE SHOULD KNOW THAT THEY CAN MAKE IT IN THEIR OWN STRUGGLES RARELY CROSSED OTHER'S LIFE AND I WAS CHOSEN AS A DUMP TRUCK PROGRAM FOR OTHERS MESS EMPTIED ON ME LIKE THIS WAS MY DREAM OR MISSION IN LIFE.

NEVER THE LESS, FIRST I WANTED MY OWN BUSINESS AS A TEE SHIRT DESIGNER. I'VE DONE FOUR OR FIVE SHIRTS BUT SINCE RELY SEEKING BUSINESS MINDED PEOPLE AS BACKERS. I WOULD ADD PUBLISHING BOOKS ABOUT MY LIFE AS THE LORD LEADS.

I'VE DONE SOME PULPIT, PRISON AND RADIO MINISTRY. A SPECIAL TEE OF MINE WHICH IS THE BIBLE IS A TKO EVERY TIME.' WITH THAT I MEANT THROUGHOUT LIFE, COME WHAT MAY, ENDURE INDIVIDUAL THOSE HARD TIMES ONTO YOUR VICTORY, NOT MINE.

SOONER OR LATER, THERE WILL BE SOME TELEVISION APPEARANCE AND MAYBE MY OWN SHOW. THE ENEMIES, THAT DEMON

APPEARANCES THROUGH PEOPLE IN ORDER TO STOP OR HINDER BUT I KNOW NO WEAPON OR WARFARE FORMED AGAINST THEE SHALL PROSPER.

THIS IS MY THIRD BOOK PUBLISHED WITH TEARS, HEARTACHES AND PAIN BUT GOD IS GREAT AND HE IS GREATLY TO BE PRAISED!

@ETHELMARGARETPOLK

WHAT MAKES ME TICK

(ABOUT THE AUTHOR)

I was a quiet person and stayed to myself with one or two girlfriends. Kids would laugh at me and call me ugly names. I had a double tooth on the side of my gums. No boys would say anything to me. I was not what they called a pretty girl that could walk beside them. Somehow, deep down on the inside, my spirit held within the depths of my heart, "beauty is only skin deep but ugly is to the bones." I wore least expensive clothes and sometimes my family did not have the money in order of getting my hair fixed but I went on to school, anyhow. Nappy headed and all growing in that attitude with a Christ like spirit.

My parents were good influences to me because they stayed together in spite of the difficult trying time. They never married but you never would have known unless you were there because he was at our side (my brother and me) all the times teaching and instructing us right from wrong. This encouraged and carried me on to this day not perfect but pressing toward the mark of the highest calling in Christ Jesus!

The only way you will become a winner is going through the get ya butt kicked school of knowledge. When you see many that put blocks in your ways scratching their heads and looking cocked eyed trying to figure out where they went wrong, the Lord will have already worked it out!

Bless you real good!

I REMEMBER WHEN WE HAD A SMALL ONE ROOM HOUSE.

AT NIGHT, MOM WOULD WALK MY BROTHER AND ME TO THE OUTDOOR TOILET BEFORE BED.

WE HAD A BIG TUB OUTSIDE AND WOULD BATHE. DAD OWNED A STORE AND BROUGHT CANDY AND ITEMS NEEDED HOME TO US. THIS WE WERE THANKFUL AT LITTLE KIDS AGES.

THAT SMALL HOUSE WENT FROM ANOTHER ROOM AND ANOTHER ROOM AND ANOTHER ROOM UNTIL THERE WERE THREE SMALL BEDROOM ROOMS, A LIVING ROOM, BATHROOM, KITCHEN AND PORCH!

WHAT A BLESSING THEN AT SMALL AGES!

AND

THE BEAT GOES ON AND ON!

WITH PRAISES!

ethel m polk

THE PROS AND CONS OF HAVING
A CHILD AT SEVENTEEN

@ethelmargaretpolk

Have you ever been talking with your girlfriend and making plans for college to later find out you are pregnant? Ironically, this happened to me in my senior year of high school. My girlfriend went on to college with the free scholarships and I was left at home counting the months before my child was born.

Here I was at seventeen and still a child having a child not knowing what I was going to do. Now, mom often talked to me but kids will be kids and that one kid time deterred some future plans for me but I had a good family to lean on and protect me. Mom right off asked me who is the daddy and where are his parents? I spoke up and told the story about what happened. I was dating a boy in school and we were allowed to go to the movies with a curfew time. Sometimes we would hold hands and maybe a kiss or two alternately. One night we went to the drive-in movies in his new car and one thing led to another. Nine month later showed the evidence. He refused to take up his responsibility but Mom was on the case to make sure that he would do the right thing. He went to the service and Mom wrote to the Chief Commander in Charge. He was sent home to straighten things out and married another girl in my class. I sat down with Mom and Dad explaining after childbirth, I would get a job to help take care of my child. This they did and smiles for their new granddaughter it was and feel they are yet smiling home with Jesus through the computer!

I came from the old school as they say where Moms knew little about talking on that personal sort of issues. S, I pained a lot but endured. These kind of pains that I had, believe I wish it on anyone because I went into seizures and blackouts as the Nurse kept telling me to bear down! Bear down! I didn't know what that was! I holler and suffered until I passed out and woke up later with babying laying besides me. One Nurse asked, "do you still want to kill me?" I looked at her strangely and she told me what had happened before I passed out. Then I smiled and laugh said no I do not still want to kill you.

After a couple of months, I went job hunting and found a car hop position. You would go to the car and take orders after which bringing it back to the car. The tips were ok! I made enough for pampers and paying Mom for child care. One night work got so hectic while taking the orders at cars with only me, I quit and found another job closer to home. Tips were not good but the owner knew my father and gave me the position as a waitress in his neighborhood bar. Through all that, Mom dranked quite a bit and would start all sorts of confusion but in the morning, she was a different person. She even put me and my child out of the house but there was a family down the street with a business and knew Mom plus Dad. We would stay there until morning and then go back to the house.

Even though I had to drop out of school after the first semester senior year, later on I got my GED. It was still like going to school for the subjects were tough and it caused me a lot of studying between changing pampers or feeding the baby but I made it! A pastor at my hometown church helped me get an apartment with reasonable rent and go on welfare so they could assist me in going to school. I could think no more about being put it! My child came first and I tried to watch out for the dangerous things against her. At times, we didn't have enough food. So, I gave the best to her and fasted plus prayed because I was taught when no one would help you in the time of need, God will!

I dated sometime and entered a college within the city but later became disinterested. At the age of two, I married a soldier and we moved upstate as I found a good job their later going to get my child from Mom. The marriage got rocky and tough! Country boy in the big city! I took all of the hell, beatings, and trouble that I was going to take after which ended up in a divorce. Some years later, I found out he was killed while we were married. I thought that speaks for the horrible times but how could he get killed and sleeping with me until the divorce? Was I sleeping with the enemy or what?

ethelmargaretpolk@

SOMEDAY! YOU'LL REMEMBER WHAT YOU BLEW

@ETHELMARGARETPOLK

I'D LIKE TO FINISH WHAT I STARTED
BUT
NOW YOU WANT TO PART
YOU TALKED IN THE HOOD AND THOUGHT
I WASN'T NOWHERE TO BE FOUND
LITTLE DID YOU KNOW I'M OUT TO STOP YOUR
BUTT FROM RUNNIN ALL OVER TOWN
GIVING FLASH REPORTS AND PUTTIN ME DOWN
I'VE COME TO REALITY THAT THIS IS A BIG FATALITY
SO, I CAN GET OFF YOUR NERVES
WATCH HOW QUICK I TURN THAT CURVE
GO HEAD AND GET WHAT YOU DESERVE
IT'S ALREADY RESERVED!
MY NEW LOVE SAID THIANKS FOR PLAYIN SILLY PRANKS
NO MORE WILL YOU HAVE ANY OF HIS DRANKS
SOMEDAY! YOU'LL REMEMBER WHAT YOU BLEW

A BREEZY LANDING THIS WILL BE

@ETHELMARGARETPOLK

HIGH IS NOT EASY IF YOU DON'T UNDERSTAND
FLYING IS ONLY INSTITUTED BY GOD'S DEMAND
CELEBRATE ELABORATELY WHEN YOU GO THROUGH ONTO
THE FINISH LINE
STARTIN BRAND NEW
WINE IS EASY, SIMPLE AND TASK MAKIN SO THAT YOU'RE
VICTORY WILL BE A SURE BLAST
RED, WHITE, AND BLUE SIMPLIFIED BY COLORS
ENSURES A SMOOTH GLIDE AWAY FROM OTHERS
HAPPY! HAPPY! GATHERIN THE SHINNIN GOLD WHICH WILL
NEVER BECOME OLD
FLOAT ON AS YOU SING WITH A SWING
PLEASURE DIVINED, REFORMED AND ALL MINE
A BREEZY LANDING THIS WILL BE

A COMMITMENT FOR TWO

@ETHELMARGARETPOLK

I NEVER WANTED OUR LOVE TO END
SO, LET'S BE MORE THAN JUST FRIENDS
YOU TELL ME WHERE TO BEGIN
OUR LOVE MUST GOOD BECAUSE JEALOUSY IS ALL OVER THE
NEIGHBORHOOD
LET OUR LOVE BECOME A LIFE TIME WITHOUT CHANGES
GIRL, I'LL TREAT YOU SO FINE WITH MUCH TENDERNESS
I CAN SEE THE MOON AND OUR STARS COMING OUT REAL
SOON
SHUTTING OUT ALL NIGHTMARES
NEVER TO FORGET OR ANYMORE REGRETS
OUR LOVE WILL BECOME HISTORY WALKING UP FROM THE
MYSTERIES
HOPING YOU KNOW WHAT I MEAN
INTEND TO KEEP YOU SO CLEAN
MY SOULMATE HAVE FINALLY COME TRUE
I CAN STOP BEING BLUE
IN PRAYER, YOU'LL ALWAYS WANT ME TOO
A COMMITMENT FOR TWO AND YOU BETTER GET READY
BECAUSE WE GOTTA MAKE A MOVE!
HURRY UP! FOR MY LOVE IS DOWN TONIGHT
THINGS ARE GONNA BE ALRIGHT
PUT ON SOME ROMANTIC MUSIC
BECAUSE
YOU SEEM SOME WHAT UP TIGHT
LONG! LONG! WILL MY LOVE BE STRONG
WE'LL BE TOGETHER EVEN AFTER THE CHILDREN ARE
GROWN
GLAD THOSE WORSE SOME MEN LEFT ME ALONE
SLOW! QUIET NIGHT! ALWAYS IN A GROOVE

GET READY BABY BECAUSE WE GOTTA MAKE A MOVE!
HIGH OR LOW, OUR LOVE WIL NEVER BE OVER
THROUGH ALL THE PHASES OF LIFE, I'VE ALWAYS BEEN
AMAZED
LET'S MAKE A SYMPHONY WHICH WILL PLEASE OUR
ANATOMY
IT HAS PROVEN TO BE GOOD THERAPY
YOU ARE STILL MY THRILL AND MAKE MY BODY CHILL!
SLOW! QUIET NIGHTS! ALWAYS IN A GROOVE!
GET READY BECAUSE WE GOTTA MAKE A MOVE!

SO SAD BUT IN THESE DAYS ARE LOW DOWN DIRTY NIGGAS

@ETHELMARGARETPOLK

*FLIP IT! DICK IT! LICK IT! WATCH OUT I'M ON MY WAY TO
KICK IT!
TOLD YA TO KEEP IT TIGHT AND I'LL
MANAGE THINGS RIGHT
NIGGAS SMILIN AND GRINNIN
MAIN ONES TRYIN TO KEEP MY POCKETS THININ
YOUR STYLE IS A WINNER AND YOU GIRLS LINES ARE
GETTING THINNER
NEVER TO BECOME A WINNER
ON THE WAY TO WEST-EAST COAST SPEAKING WITH MY
MAN
THAT'LL FILL YA POCKETS WITH CASH AND FINE GEMS
KEEP THE LYRICS RUNNIN LINE BY LINE ON THE WAY TO
OUR FINISH LINE
CAUSE THEY JUST ALL MINE!
YEAH! THAT'S RIGHT
GOT DAM ON TIME!
ON THE WAY TO WINNIN AND MOVIN OUT ALL THAT'S
THININ
POP MY TRIGGER TO THOSE WHO WON'R HEAR
KEEP STANIN THEIR BLOCKIN
SITTIN ME UP FOR A RIP OFF
SET DOWN THEY'LL NEVER BE FOUND
MUM WILL BE THE WORD ALL OVER TOWN
THEN WE'LL BECOME THICK KNOWIN I DIDN'T ONLY WANT
JUST A LICK
WANTIN TO BE WITH YOU IS SUCH A THRILL
EACK TIME I THINK BRINGS ME CHILLS!*

BABY, I'M HERE NOW

@ETHELMARGARETPOLK

IF THE WAY WE FEEL IS REAL
THEN THINGS SAID WON'T BECOME A BIG DEAL
A LOVE STORY NEVER TOLD
WILL BE OUR HIGHEST GOAL
EVERYTHING WILL TURN OUT RIGHT
CAUSE YOU'VE STRAIGHTENED OUT
THINGS WITHOUT A FIGHT
NOW, I REALLY CAN SEE AND I'M
HAPPY LIKE A BUMBLING BEE
JUST TAKE THE TIME TO BELIEVE
YOU'LL BEGAN TO RELIEVE
WE'RE ON OUR WAY UP THROUGH THIS BITTER CUP
I'M HERE NOW
BABY, I'M HERE NOW
YOU TURNED, NOW TAKE OVER MY
CONTROLS AND I WILL FOLLOW
YOUR SWEET DEMANDS
MOST OF ALL, EACH LOVE COMMAND
NO MORE WORRIES FOR I'LL BE THERE
IN A HURRY TO THIS VERY
DAY
BABY! BABY! I'M HERE NOW

NOW, I'M STANDIN UP ON MY OWN TWO FEET

@ETHELMARGARET

I'M WOMAN ENOUGH TO KNOW MANY OF MY DUTIES
SO, WHY ARE YOU OUT THERE MESSIN WITH THOSES
THINK THEY SO FINE CUTIES?
NOT LETTIN ME HELP BECAUSE MANY NIGHTS I'VE NOT
SLEPT SINCE YOU LEFT
THIS IS NOT THE WAY WE PLANNED NOR HONOURED EACH
OTHERS COMMAND
SEEM LIKE ALL THAT IS DEMANDS
THE ONLY WAY FOR ME TO GET SOME OF YOUR LOVE IS
TIP! TAP! AND STAND ON MY KNEES BEGGIN YOU PLEASE!
SO, OUR MINDS CAN BE AT EASE BY BOTH GETTING RELIEF
STOPPIN SORROW AND GRIEF
I'M GONNA STANDUP ON MY OWN TWO FEET IN THE MIST
OF ALL THIS HEAT!
YOU ARE NOT LOVING ME WITH ALL YOUR HEART IS WHY
WE FELL APART
I'M STILL NOT WEAK BUT THE TEMPTATION IS STRONGER
AND I'M NO TOY
JUST HUMAN TRYIN TO GET YOU TO UNDERSTAND
I'M THE ONE THAT CAN HANDLE ALL YOUR DEMANDS
WE COULD HAVE BEEN THE ONLY TWO IN THIS WORLD
WITH TROUBLES ALL AROUND BUT OUR LOVE WOULD
HAVE KEPT US BOUND WITH NO PLACE TO BREAK OR NOT
EVEN A MOMENT OF HEARTACHES
NOW I GOT TO STAND UP ON MY OWN TWO FEET
BABY! BABY! NOW I GOT TO STANDUP ON MY OWN TWO
FEET!

PLEASE TELL ME MORE ABOUT YOUR FAITH

@ethelmargaret

FAITH IS THE EVIDENCE OF THINGS NOT SEEN
REALLY DON'T SEEM SO MEAN
WHERE ARE YOU GOING AND TELL ME WHAT
YOU'RE DOING
MYSTERY IS IN YOUR MIND
I WANT THINGS TO GO REAL FINE
STOP LISTENING TO OTHERS FOR I DON'T HAVE
ANOTHER
DEEP DOWN IN MY HEART I DON'T WANT TO PART
PLEASE TELL ME MORE ABOUT YOUR FAITH
DOORS SEEM TO OPEN AND NEVER SHUT
SEE THAT YOU CAME OUT OF A LITTLE HUT
IF YOU WANT TO CHANGE, BABY I'LL BE THE ONE
TO REARRANGE
PLEASE TELL ME MORE ABOUT YOUR FAITH

SEEK GOD BECAUSE HE'S NEAR

@ethelmargaretpolk

It is time to kick back in your sack
Honestly
And seek God because he's near
The Lord will stand by you even if it's wrong
But
You must remember this it want be too long
Running away from your test before you've done your
best
Will only make your enemy continue to be a pest
Stumble! Bumblin! Will disappear!
If you honestly seek the Lord!
Let me say this one more time!
If you honestly seek the Lord askin him to come near
Then your worries will cease and get a good release
Lonely sometime, then out of the blue!
Will come God's relief
Removing that load and dispensing it back to who it
belongs
Kick back! Glory!
Glory! Glory! Kick back! In your sack hon-est-ly
And
Seek God because he's near
He's near! He's near!
Seek God because he's near

I WILL REALLY ALWAYS LOVE THEE

@ ETHELMARGARET

TO MAKE THINGS COME ALIVE, YOU
GOT TO BE ALREADY REVISED
BUT
I LOOKED FOR YOUR ATTENTION AND
EVERYTHING MENTIONED
PARADISE IS HERE-SO GLAD THAT YOU'RE REAL NEAR
ALWAYS DO SOMETHING NICE AND SOMETIME
TAKE SOMEONE ELSE ADVICE
BIG WHEELS WILL KEEP ON TURNIN PLUS
MY LOVE WILL STILL BE BURNIN
KEEP THINGS FOR REAL WHEN WE MAKE THIS DEAL
I AM A TYPICAL FEMALE THAT NEEDS
SOME ATTENTION TOO
THIS MAYBE TO YOU SOMETHING NEW!
BEEN LOOKIN FOR A REAL MALE WITH GOOD ACTIONS!
BUT MANY ARE THE SAME - JUST KEEP
PLAYIN SILLY OLD FASHION GAMES
YOU WILL BE MY BEGININ TO THE END
ALSO, KEEPING ISSUES AMENDED AS THEY
BEGIN THROUGH THE THICK AND
THIN
FEEL LIKE I'VE KNOWN YOU DOWN
THROUGHOUT THE YEARS
SO, FAMILIAR TO ME AND NO FEARS
THERE'S SOMETHING SPECIAL ABOUT YOUR KISS
SHOULD I LOSE OUT, MANY REGRETS AND MUCH MISSED
IN YOUR ARMS IS WHERE I WANT TO BE
JUST LEAVE THINGS NOW UP TO ME

BECAUSE
I WILL REALLY ALWAYS LOVE THEE
I LOVE THEE!
I WILL REALLY ALWAYS LOVE THEE

THEM NIGGAS ALMOST HAD ME BEAT!

@ethelmargaret

Baby, I come back to confess and get you out of all this mesh
Stress no more cause as I look at that glow on your face
Finally convince me I gotta get you away from this place
You're the one with listenin ears nor discouraging any of my careers
Ready to cease and get me some release
Glory to the most high cause I got a second chance for your continual
Sweet romance
With all the dirt and hindrances removed
Allowin us to groove
Going to put some money in your pocket
Cause unexpectedly you protected me
Down in the midst of all the heat
Them niggas almost had me beat
I got a second chance for your continual sweet romance
With all the dirt and hindrances removed
Allowing us to groove
Them niggas almost had me beat baby! Baby!
Them niggas almost had me beat!

CHRIST! OUR LORD AND SAVIOUR WILL RELIEVE IN DUE TIME

@ETHELMARGARETPOLK

HAPPINESS BRINGS ABOUT JOY
IF
YOU GET IT FROM OUR LORD AND SAVIOUR JESUS CHRIST
NOT EVER AGAIN TO THINK TWICE
SHOULD NOT HAVE BEEN TROUBLE
BUT
IT SETS A CHAIN ORDER OF DEMAND
CONCLUDING WITH THE BIBLE
ARRIVING AT ANYTIME OR DATE!
NEVER LATE!
THE LORD IS NEVER! EVER LATE!
COME CLOSER TO YOUR FAMILY
AND
BEGAN TO BELIEVE
ONLY THEN WILL THE LORD RELIEVE
THEN, ANY DATE WILL NOT MATTER
COME CLOSER TO YOUR FAMILY
AND
BEGAN TO BELIEVE
ONLY THEN WILL THE LORD RELIEVE
CHRIST IS OUR ONLY HOPE
SO, TAKE THE TIME AND KEEP SAYING NO TO DOPE
GLORY HALLEUIAH! IN DUE TIME
CHRIST LORD AND SAVIOUR WILL RELIEVE IN DUE TIME
IN DUE TIME
CHRIST! OUR LORD AND SAVIOUR
WILL RELIEVE IN DUE TIME

AN ALMIGHTY GOD IS YET ALIVE

@ETHEL

LET'S START TRAININ UP YOUR CHILD AS GOD WANTS TO DO
STEP BY STEP WITH SPIRITUAL GUIDANCE WILL THEN RESIDE
AND NO ON ELSE WILL TAKE THEM FOR A RIDE
TALK ABOUT GOD'S EXAMPLE OF WHAT'S REALLY GOING ON
SO THEY WANT BE DEFEATED BY ANYTHING THAT'S WRONG
THE ENEMY WILL HAVE TO BE LONG GONE
KING JESUS BORE YOUR BATTLES A LONG TIME AGO
SO THE WORLD CAN SEE HE STILL EXIST AMONG THIS MIST
CALL HIM WHAT EVER YOU WANT HIS NAME
LIFE IS NOT A GAME
THE ANSWER STILL REMAINS
AN ALL MIGHTY GOD IS YET ALIVE AND FULL OF POWER EACH
AND EVERY HOUR THAT WILL TAKE YOU ON TO VICTORY
AN ALMIGHTY GOD IS YET ALIVE

I STILL LOVE YOU

@ethelmargaret

I GUESS YOU'RE STRONG AND WANT
ME TO LEAVE YOU ALONE
NO ONE YOU NEED
NOT A FRIEND INDEED
YOU TOLD ME TO KEEP CLEAR
AND I HEARD NOT TO COME NEAR
KNOW YOU'LL NEVER ADMIT
TIME BROUGHT THAT CHANGE
YOU WANT TO QUIT
JUST SAY THE WORDS FOR I STILL LOVE YOU
JUST SAY THE WORDS FOR I STILL LOVE YOU
PEOPLE CAN CEASE THE PRESSURE AND
STOP GIVING ME LECTURES
GOSSIP WAS SAID JUST FOR THRILLS
YET THE FACT OF MATTER IS STILL
TAKE YOU TIME AND SEE THAT YOU'RE STILL MINE
WHEN YOU'RE FEELING BETTER AND
NOT UNDER THE WEATHER
I WANT YOU BACK IN MY LIFE
JUST SAY THE WORDS FOR I STILL LOVE YOU

COME ON BABY, LET'S JUST LIVE

@ethel

Let's start a new making life fresh as the morning dew
Each day will stop being a hustle
For time is at hand
So we can fill our companies demand
Much to do
No work finding cause it's in front of you
I kindly see that you survived
Many were surprised
As darkness closes in let's stick by each other to the bitter
end
Your wait is over because patient you did show
Girl, come on and let's go
I'll move you away from that spot
Your enemies have made it real hot
Be my lady and I am your man
As spirits rises they can see you in my arms safe from all
harm
Let's take time for each other everyday
Work will still be here after one of us have passed away
Getting things together in spite of the weather
I got a lot of love to give
So come on baby, let's just live
I got a lot of love to give
So come on baby, let's just live

DO YOU REALLY WANT TO JAM?

@ethelmargaret

Before askin my name-tell me your game
Is this real or fake? What's the word for heaven sake?
Or does it matter, I don't know
Just let the feelin flow
I see your face all over the place
Come let's discuss and not make a real big fuss
I'm good lookin and you better get me hooked
So I can flip a page at this age
Or maybe get engaged
A diamond ring would really shine plus wishin that you were truly mine not
carin where you been but it's about what I'm gonna send so we can begin
If you can't see your way out baby call me and I'll tell you what's it all about
I'm about to take you down to the bookin so you can get hooked
See you started payin the cost in being your own boss
Do you really want to jam?

DON'T LEAVE ME NOW

@ETHELMARGARET

I stand here listening to my life go by and at times-I wonder why try
Finally got the nerve to move on-leavin you alone
After we lay, maybe I might want to stay
Love surely don't love-just only from above
Love forgot we use to be fine
Only just a matter of time
Our poetry will always rhyme
Love oh love of mine!
Take no others advice not thinkin twice
Please tell me yes and I will not go
Don't leave me now

DRUNK AGAIN!

@ETHELMPOLK

If you just wanna play
Then go another way
Layin out after dawn
Body lookin like a fawn
Threw money on the floor
As
I walked out the door
DRUNK AGAIN!
Guess! I'll never win
I'm filled with lots of troubled gin
So! You better get here on the double
Didn't have to end like this
Just all that money I missed
Feel like shootin some ugly witch
Maybe some lootin the way things going down
Someone ain't gonna be around
Got nothing to loose
Cause
I always been abused
Can't sleep or eat
Under too much heat
Any day, you'll find me
Dead as can be
Fucked! Sucked! And licked!
Maybe, even wearing a dick!
Yesterday's gone

Maybe tomorrow! You'll leave me alone!
Pumpin shots in me just maybe my goal
Who is the one that will take that first roll?
Tired of this old life's toll
Drunk again!

FROM THE INSIDE OUT

@ethel m polk

Christmas is a time that should be shown from the inside out
Without any shadow of doubt
That's told of the scripture embedded deep down in your mind
Will become steady
But
Always in a good frame of the mind
Inside season comes a dwelling of sun light
Relieving all your fights
A over whelming of the holy spirit brings confidence of love always by your
side when getting old and physical abilities began to not work
Because
We'll be together enduring the clouds and storms
Remembering back of how we never left each other's side
Thanking God for his holy words sealed within with when neither of us
ran away at the sight of a little whim
From the inside out
Thank God!
Praise his holy name!
Thanking God from the inside out
The inside out
From the inside out!

GO HEAD BROTHER! LET YA MOMMA DO HER THANG!

@ETHELMARGARETPOLK

NO MATTER WHERE EVER YOU GO
LEARN EXACTLY WHAT YOU'LL NEED TO KNOW
LIFE IS A STRUGGLE
BUT
MANY HAVE KEPT IT UNDER COVER BOUT SO MANY LOVERS
ONE, TWO, THREE, OUT OF BEDS
GIVIN UP PLENTY HEAD
NOT CONSIDERIN WHAT KIND OF LIFE THEY LED
MY POCKETS WERE EMPTY AND THAT FOOD AT HOME I JUST
COULD NOT EAT
SAYIN!
IT IS OUR HERITAGE! SON
SO!
PLEASE DO NOT RUIN!
THAT IS WHY YOUR POOR PEOPLE
HAVE BEEN UNDER THE GUN
ALL OF A SUDDEN, MY BROTHER! SISTER AND MOTHER!
WANTED TO BECOME ONE OF MY LOVERS
YOU GOT TO BE INSANE OR FULL OF UNAUTHORIZED DOPE
WITH NO HOPE
BETTER FOR ME TO GO A DIFFERENT WAY
MUCH QUICKER FROM BLOCK TO BLOCK
I'M HEARIN THE SAME THANG
GO HEAD BROTHER!

LET YA MOMMA DO HER THANG1
HEY NOW!
GO RIGHT ON!
ON AND ON! MY BROTHER!
GO HEAD BROTHER! LET YA MOMMA DO HER THANG!

WHEN YOU SHUT ME OFF REMEMBER THE HURT AND GIVE ME THIS ONE MORE CHANCE

@ethelmargaret

Should we become together, there are issues you must
know before you find out and decide to go
My love is real- it's not a one day feel nor a childish thrill
Release all of your love unto me because I'll make you happy as can be
Not only the latest fashion but each filled with passion
and desire so you'll know that admire
Walkin away will not profit much but just the two of us losin touch- I
never been with someone who understood my each and every needs
They would always see and not take heed, smilin, drankin and
puffin on some weed-after going down this desolate road paying
a heavy toll getting directly to you, thankin God and prayin
we'll never be through but on to better things startin new
When you shut me off remember the hurt and give me this one more chance

WILL YOU BE THE ONE TO BREAK THEM?

@ETHELMARGARET

Not lookin for love or ever thinkin it would come
But
You're now my number one
Out of the clear blue of skies came you ministerin to my utter most of dream
As I travel, I'm highly esteemed
Rich nor poor or askin for nothing but I must admire
Askin that you consider me one of your number one desires
Promises are made but will you be the one to break them
Shuttin the door reconsiderin not wantin anymore
Alone I've always been hopin I'm about to win because
you seem the only one I can most depend
Promise are made but will you be the one to break them
Baby baby tell me please will you be the one to break them?

WILL YOU LET ME SHARE YOUR MIRROR AND BECOME AS ONE?

@ethelmargaret

AFTER MY HEAD'S CLEAR, I'M STILL
WISHING YOU WERE NEAR
SHOULD HAVE TALKED ABOUT MY LOVE FOR YOU DEAR
JUST AS I OPENED MY EYES TO BE REAL
YOU WALKED OUT TO ANOTHER DEAL
GUESS I WON'T APPEAR
KNOWING THAT I LOST AND BEGAN TO PAY THE COST
I FIND NO REASON TO LIE
YOU'RE WHY I WANTED TO LIVE
AND
WHATEVER IT TOOK I'D GIVE
IF YOU LET ME SHARE YOUR MIRROR AND BECOME AS ONE
EVERY WAY I TURN, YOU'RE THERE IN RETURN
THROUGHOUT THE YEARS, I'LL GO ON AND FIGHT THE
TEARS
WISHED! ASKING!
WILL YOU LET ME SHARE YOUR MIRROR
AND BECOME AS ONE?

WHERE DID YOUR LOVE COME FROM?

CARS! DIAMOND RINGS OR HOMES!
DO NOT MAKE MY HEART SING
IT IS JUST THAT PURE LOVE YOUR BRING
I NEED YOUR BODY
SO BABY!
TELL ME WHAT TO DO
ALL THAT MATTERS IS FOR YOU TO LOVE ME
THERE WILL NEVER BE ANOTHER TO KEEP THESE FEELINGS
COMING
I WILL ALWAYS BE HERE FOR YOUR WANTING
NO STRESSING OR PRESSURE
JUST STRAIGHT LOVE MEASURES
FOR YOU ARE MY LIFE'S TREASURE
A CONFIDENCE THAT COME WITH MOODS
WHICH WILL NEVER BECOME RUDE
YOU'RE EVERYTHING A MAN WANTS IN A WOMAN
AND
KEEPING ALL THINGS COMMON
ONE IN A MILLION
TOPS BILLIONS
WHERE DID YOUR LOVE COME FROM?
BABY! BABY! PLEASE TELL ME!
WHERE DID YOUR LOVE COME FROM?

@ethelmpolk

WILL YOU THINK AGAIN ABOUT OUR LOVE?

@ETHELMARGARET

I'LL STAY TO THE END AND SEE IF WE CAN MEND OUR LOVE
WE ONCE SHARED SUCH A HAPPILY PAIR
HOW AWFUL WERE YOUR WORDS
ABOUT MANY THINGS HEARD
GUESS, I'LL HIT THE DOOR CAUSE
YOU'VE BECOME SUCK A BORE
BEAT YOU TO THE PUNCH-DON'T WORRY ABOUT LUNCH
WILL YOU THINK AGAIN ABOUT OUR LOVE?
LOOKING AT THE SIGNS-I RESISTED IT ALL FOR
REMEMBERING HOW WE HAD A BALL
PLEASE STOP PLAYING ME FOR A FOOL-I
DON'T HAVE TO GO TO SCHOOL
YOU ARE THE BLAME IN DOING SILLY GAMES
IT WILL ONLY BE RIGHT NOW-IF YOU'LL LOVE ME ANYHOW
WILL YOU THINK AGAIN ABOUT OUR LOVE?

YOU AND I IN A DREAM

@ETHEL MARGARET POLK

YOU'RE THE CENTER OF MY DREAMS
LIKE CHOCOLATE ICE CREAM
WAKING ME UP WITH SWEAT
HAVEN'T SEEN YOU YET
MY LOVE WILL NEVER END
ALWAYS READY TO MEND
IT IS JUST YOU WHO SATISFIES ME
AROUND AND HAPPY AS I CAN BE
YOU SATISFY ALL MY THRILLS
BRINGING ABOUT SO MUCH WARM CHILLS
I'LL PAY ALL YOUR BILLS
JUST TO BE WITH YOU
AND
NEVER BECOME THROUGH
AFTER YOU'RE GONE AND I AM ALONE
WAITING PATIENTLY BY THE PHONE
DON'T WAKE ME UP
FOR I LOVE THIS BITTER CUP
YOU AND ME
BABY!
YOU AND ME IN A DREAM
IN A DREAM
YOU AND ME, BABY
YOU AND ME IN A DREAM

YOU ARE MY BEST FRIEND

@ethelmargaret

SOMETHINGS MAY BE MISSIN BUT
TO US WE'RE NOT INSISTIN
OUR LOVE IS JUST TO BE
ONLY YOU AND ME
YOU'RE MINE, LADY FOREVER AND ALL THE TIME
TOGETHER WE'LL WIN KNOWIN THAT
YOU WILL BE THERE TO DEFEND
FROM START TO THE END BABY YOU ARE MY BEST FRIEND
FEEL THE MUSIC IN YOUR EARS
JUST LIKE A SYMPHONY REAL NEAR
I'LL ALWAYS BE HERE WHEN YOU NEED
A REAL TRUE FRIEND, INDEED
ANY WHERE YOU GO OR WHAT WE DO
THERE'LL BE NO OTHER LOVE
JUST YOU FROM START TO THE FINISH
YOU ARE MY BEST FRIEND

I DON'T WANNA BREATHE UNLESS IT'S WITH YOU

@ETHELMARGARETPOLK

I'M NOT A CHILD ANYMORE AS YOU KNOW
SO, LET US TALK ABOUT THINGS THE
WAY WE'D LIKE FOR IT TO GO
THEN, WE BOTH WON'T LOSE OUR MIND WONDERIN
IF IT'S TRULY LOVE OR JUST A PHYSICAL ATTRACTION
THAT BRINGS ABOUT TEMPORARY REACTIONS
I DON'T WANNA BREATHE UNLESS IT'S WITH YOU
NEVER IN MY LIFE HAVE I FELT SO SECURE
WRAPPED UP IN YOUR ARMS DAILY
SUPPLYING ALL THAT YOU NEED
EVEN IF IT'S JUST TO SMOKE SOME WEED
NO MORE SINKIN IN QUICK SAND
UNDER OTHERS COMMANDS
LET'S GET A PERSONAL UNDERSTANDIN
ABOUT EACH OTHERS BELIEF
AND
TOGETHER SOLVE FOR A PERFECT RELIEF
WE'LL WIPE THE TEARS FROM EACH OTHERS EYES
WITH GENTILE SMILES WHICH MEANS SO MUCH
I DON'T WANNA BREATHE UNLESS IT'S WITH YOU

BABY, NOW I GOT TO LEAVE YOU ALONE!

@ETHELMARGARETPOLK

WE SOMETIME FALL IN LOVE AND NOT
OFTEN IT'S NOT FROM HEAVEN ABOVE
HEARTS BROKEN WITH WORDS LEFT UNSPOKEN
DRIFTING ON THROUGH OLD MEMORIES LEFT BY YOU
I WANTED TO BE LIVING AND GIVING JUST
FOR EACH MOMENT OF YOUR LOVE
BUT
I'VE LOST MY WAY AND JUST NEEDED
A SPECIAL PLACE TO STAY
REMEMBERING WHEN WE BEGAN, I NEVER
THOUGHT THINGS WOULD COME TO THIS END
I TRIED TO MAKE YOU CHOOSE, BABY
NOW I'M ABOUT TO LOSE OR BABY, NOW
I GOT TO LEAVE YOU ALONE
WILL YOU MAKE A CHANGE OR REARRANGE
BECAUSE SINCE YOU'RE NOT AROUND
A NEW LOVE I'VE FOUND
I REALLY WANTED SOME OF YOUR TIME
JUST TO KEEP THIS THOUGHT ON YOUR MIND!
I KNOW! YOU KNOW! AND THE WORLD KNOW
THAT YOU HAVE BEEN DOING WRONG
TAKING ME FOR A FOOL
BETTER GO BACK TO SCHOOL!
BABY, NOW I GOT TO LEAVE YOU ALONE
DON'T CALL ME ON THE PHONE
BECAUSE I'LL ALWAYS BE GONE
BABY, NOW I GOT TO LEAVE YOU ALONE!

I'D LIKE TO BE YOUR SUGAR DADDY

@ETHELMARGARETHILL

I'D LIKE TO BE YOUR SUGAR DADDY
KNOW YA WILL MAKE ME REAL HAPPY
YOUR STYLE, BABY, TURNS ME ON AND AWAY WITH MY PAIN
TOWARD MORE TO GAIN
LOOKING AT THE SUN SHINE THROUGH
YOUR FACE AFTER THE RAIN
CAN YOU FEEL MY MAGIC CLOSING UP ALL YOUR TRAGICS?
BUILDING UP TRUST IN ME IS A MUST
AND
LETS JUST GO HEAD AND FUSS GETTING
THAT OUT OF THE WAY
BECAUSE THIS IS TURNING OUT TO BE A VERY GOOD DAY
START THINKIN OF ME AS YOUR DADDY TO
START CLEANIN OUT YOUR MIND
KNOWIN IT WOULD BE JUST A MATTER OF TIME
IT'S MY DUTY CAUSE YOU'RE A REAL CUTIE
NO MOE KNOCKIN COLD YOUR PLANS
GET READY FOR THAT HOUSE AND ALL THAT LAND
GLADNESS WILL REMOVE YOUR SADNESS
I'M THE ONE YOU BLESSED AND RELIEVED MY STRESS
NOW! MY PAIN IS GONE AND I STAND STRONG THROUGH
ALL THOSE BLOWS AND ONTO JAIL THEY GO!
I'D LIKE TO BE YOUR SUGAR DADDY, YES SIR!
YES MAM! I'D LIKE TO BE YOUR SUGAR DADDY!
STRAIGHT UP! I'LL BE GOOD!

LET EVERYONE KNOW IN THE HOOD

FILL THE HOUSE UP WITH KIDS CAUSE THEY KEPT TRYIN TO
KEEP YOU HID
SEE THAT YOU'LL STAY COMMITTED
WATCH OUT NIGGA! YOU'RE BOUT TO
GET HIT! ALL UPSIDE YA HEAD
FOR TRYIN TO GET IN MY BED
AND SWAYIN ME TO GET MISLED
DON'T YA SEE THE SIGN! THAT GIRL IS ALL MINE?
SHE GOT MY HEART AND I'M KEEPIN HER AWAY FROM FEAR
NOW THAT MY GIRL REALLY IS NEAR
CLEARIN ALL ISSUES AND THROWIN AWAY THE TISSUES
UP TO THE HIGHEST LEVEL! LEAVIN THEM
WH THOUGHT THEY WERE SO CLEVER
FORGET IT NIGGAS! NEVER! EVER! NEVER!
DOWN UNDER THE SHEETS, BETWEEN YA LEGS
I WILL EAT EVERYTIME WE MEET
REACHIN OUT MY HAND HOPIN YOU'LL ACCEPT
SEEIN THAT ALL PROMISES WILL BE KEPT
FIRST TIME THIS WAY I'VE FELT MY HEART MELT
AND
A CALM PEACE I'VE NEVER FELT
YOU'RE THE ESSENCE OF MY PRESENCE!
LAY BACK AND ROLL UP A BLUNT
NO LONGER BABY WILL YOU HAVE TO HUNT
I'D LIKE TO BE YOUR SUGAR DADDY!
YES, I WOULD BABY
SURE WOULD LIKE TO BE YOUR SUGAR DADDY
I'D LIKE TO BE YOUR SUGAR DADDY!

YOU STOLE MY SHOW

@ethelmpolk

*never had a problem-no need for someone to solve
them
UNTIL!
sitting at home alone one night
listening to a funky music band beat
jumped up and started to groovin!
humpin! Bumpin! and swingin to an automatic stop!
baby, on you my eyes locked
your moves were nice and slow
You Stole My Show!
i was somewhat behind-lost all down in the line
but
you put up such a good fight
had to come up and love you with all my might
come, let me change your name
in my body you will stay as i frame
you always will be the same
You Stole The Show!
Baby, YOU STOLE MY SHOW!*

YOU'LL ALWAYS BE THE ONE HOLDING MY HEART

IS IT TIME AT HOME WHAT WE NEED?
WHAT ABOUT OUR LOVE INDEED?
WE HAVE A BEAUTIFUL STORY WITH GOD'S GLORY
PARTING WON'T CHANGE OR MAKE THINGS REARRANGE
LET'S NOT DEPART AND BREAK EACH OTHER'S HEART
LET ME STAY BESIDE YOU THROUGH THE STORM
TO KEEP YOUR BODY WARM AND SAFE FROM ALL HARM
WE CAN TAKE HARD TIMES TOGETHER
THEN COME OUT LIKE SUNNY WEATHER
I MET SOMEONE ELSE AND THOUGHT EVERYTHING WOULD
WORK OUT FINE
ONLY FOUND OUT THAT WE WERE NOT THE LOVING KIND
IN MY HEART, YOU'RE STILL STAMPED AS MINE
I KNOW I'M THE BLAME FOR THINKING REAL LAME AND
PLAYING THE SILLY GAMES BUT YOU'LL ALWAYS BE THE ONE
HOLDING MY HEART! MY HEART! MY HEART! BABY, YOU'LL
ALWAYS BE THE ONE HOLDING MY HEART

@em

A-REAL-EASY -PREY

@ETHELMARGARETPOLK

LIFE HAD GOTTEN SO TRAGIC
BUT!
AT THE PULL OFF OF MY HAT PRODUCED MAGIC
THE REMEMBRANCE OF MY FAMILY THAT I HAD
AND HARDLY DIDN'T KNOW
WHILE MY BUSINESS SLOWLY DEPARTED
NOONE SHOWED A HEART
JUST CONSTANTLY SAYING GIMME! GIMME
ME EVERYTHING YOU GOT!
THEN YOU WON'T BECOME SO HOT
IF YOU JUST WILL NOT LOSE YA WILL
BABY! YOU'LL BECOME MY BIG STEAL!
CLOSING OFF ON A REAL BIG DEAL!
WITH FAME AND FORTUNE! ONTO THE MASTER GAME
BETTER HOLD ON TIGHT AND QUICK
SOMEWHERE DOWN THE LINE, I WILL
LET YOU SUCK MY DICK
KNOWIN NOW YOU'RE NOT AS THEY SAID!
NO MORE WILL I WANT TO BECOME YOUR BOSS
AFTER YOU PAID A REAL BIG COST
A REAL EASY PREY THAT YOU DON'T HAVE TO PAY
A REAL EASY PREY!
HIP HOPPIN AND SICO ROCKIN!
A REAL EASY PREY!

A REAL NIGGA FELL IN LOVE

@ethelmpolk

Let me know what ya want and it will be done
If
I have to put someone under the gun
No help or any amends baby
I'm going on through with you to the bitter end
Pullin my pants up and not letting them sag
No more will you look like a forgotten hag
I'm on fire and waitin for your drill
Drinking good wine
While havin a good time
Together we'll go on up to the highest peak
Thanks for standin still and continuing
To be meek
Ignorin any fate
You're my soul mate
Ain't tryin to be rude
But
You are my dude
Or
Just in a bad mood
Love to laugh and no I'm not gay

LET OTHERS CONTINUE TO BE ON THEIR WAY

REALLY GLAD TOO WE MET
LET'S BREAK OUT IN SOME SWEAT
A REAL NIGGA FELL IN LOVE

ALWAYS SOMEONE ELSE DADDY AND POPS

@ETHELMARGARETPOLK

MOM SAID POPS LAID WITH EVERY GIRL IN TOWN
AND
ALWAYS PUT HIS FAMILY DOWN
TO GO FOR A DRINK AND DOPE
NOT EVEN TAKING A MOMENT TO THINK OUT THE DAY
LOST WITHOUT HOPE
NEVER STOPPING TO TAKE THE CHANCE OR BEGAN
TO REARRANGE HIS STEPS THE OTHER WAY
SO THAT WE COULD SEE HIM ONE DAY
TALKS! WHISPERS! ARE ALL WE HEAR
AS THEY CALLED HIM SOME KIND OF NERD
ROLLING AROUND IN SHEETS NOT CARING
WHO OR WHAT HE WOULD MEET
COLLECTING WIVES AND CHILDREN WERE HIS GAME
MOM ALWAYS HELD HER HEAD DOWN IN SUCH A SHAME
TRYING TO PROTECT US FROM THE BAD AND
ALL THE WOMEN PLUS MEN THAT HE HAD
AS HE DIED, I DIDN'T CRY BECAUSE HE REALLY DIDN'T TRY
ALWAYS SOMEONE ELSE DADDY AND POPS!

BUILD OUR LOVE TO THE SKIES AND NEVER LET GO

@ethelmargaret

Love can become a song that will forever last even if you go out like a blast
It will continue to be a thing of the past
I got what you need once in a life time relief
Those dreams can be real feelings with chills and oh! Boy! The thrills!
The best of life you shall have-no more grabbing
or takin on the way to number one
Selected from the shuttin of doors tryin to keep me
from proceedin on with you to brand new
Talk to me about love
It's been a sex drive with nothing but the walkin out into another's arm
Let's build our love to the skies and never let go

BECOME MY WOMAN TONIGHT

@ETHELMPOLK

WE MAYBE AT OUR LAST-SO LET NOT THE TIME PAST
RUN TO EACH OTHER REAL FAST SO THAT TOUCHING
AND HOLDING WILL CONTINUE TO BE OUR GOAL
A SURRENDER OF LOVE SO SWEET WHICH
WILL WORK OUT VERY NEAT
SOMETHING, NO ONE ELSE CAN BEAT
GOD CREATED US AS ONE
OUR HEART WILL BEAT EACH TIME THAT WE MEET
AND
I'LL BE YOUR MAN AT ANY DEMAND
PLEASE BECOME MY WOMAN AS I SPEAK THE COMMAND
MY ARMS ARE PURE AND SECURE
SIMPLE AND AT EASE-READY TO PLEASE BEYOND
ALL MEASURES-FULL OF DELIGHTFUL PLEASURE
PRECIOUS IS THE TIME
SIT DOWN AND DRINK WITH ME SOME WINE
A MOMENT FULL OF TREASURE AS THE MORNING APPEARS
WITH YOU STILL NEAR SAYING GOOD MORNING DEAR
YOUR WISH WILL ALWAYS BE GRANTED
ANYWHERE ON THIS PLANET
THE MAGIC OF LOVE HAVE BEGUN
SURELY YOU ARE NOT GOING TO RUN
BECOME MY WOMAN TONIGHT

BETTER MAKE YOUR SECOND A BLAST

@ETHELMARGARET

RAIN CAN POUR EVEN IF YOU'RE STILL INDOORS
WET WITH THE TEARS OF DIFFERENT PEOPLE
RUNNIN ROUND WITH NO PLACE TO GO
THAT THOUGHT SHOULD HAVEN BEEN STUDIED
BEFORE YOU TOOK ALL THAT MONEY LYIN
SAYIN I WILL ALWAYS BE YOUR HONEY!
NOW, YOU'RE SCARED AT WHO YOU FINALLY
SEE NO LONGER HAPPY NOR GLEE
SOMEWHERE IN THE BIBLE WHICH YOU THREW
ASIDE NOTED "MONEY" IS THE ROOT OF EVIL
SOMEHOW YOU FORGOT
THIS WOULD HAVE BEEN IN FIGHTING
AGAINST YOUR WON TROUBLES
INSTEAD OF TRYIN TO THROW THEM OFF THE
WRONG WAY REQUIRING MAM TO PAY THE COST
RECONSIDER NOW BEFORE YOU SINK UNDER
AND BEGIN TO PLEAD FOR JESUS
HELP! HOLDIN UP BOTH OF YOUR HANDS
BUT HE'LL BE RIGHT THERE BEFORE YOU'RE AT YOUR LAST
BETTER MAKE YOUR SECOND TIME A REAL JESUS BLAST!

NO DOUBT I NEED YOUR LOVE

@ETHELMARGARETPOLK
FELT LIKE DYIN, SCREAMIN PLEASE LET ME OUT
LIFE'S BEEN NOTHIN
NOT EVEN A SHOUT
I TRY TO COMFORT MYSELF SAYIN, I'M A GOOD
GUY BUT IN MY HEART, I WONDER WHY
GOOD WOMEN RUN FROM ME MAKIN
LOVE UNHAPPY AS CAN BE
ABOUT TO LOSE MY MIND
BABY, I'M HERE FOR YOU TO FIND
NO DOUBT I NEED YOUR LOVE
SOMEWHERE THERE'S A LOVE WAITIN
FOR ME TO START DATIN
JUST MAYBE, SHE WILL BE MY MATE
THANK GOD, IT WILL NOT BE TOO LATE
A LOVE SWEET AND DIVING PLUS TRULY WILL BE MINE
REALITY WILL ONCE AGAIN SHINE
SKIES WILL BECOME BLUE CAUSE YOU'RE
THE ONE FOR ME TO BE TRUE
NO DOUBT I NEED YOUR LOVE
DO! DO! DO!
BABY, REALLY I DO
NO DOUBT I NEED YOUR LOVE

YOU'RE EVERYTHING IN A MAN'S HOPES

@ETHELMARGARETPOLK

I LOVE YOU THE MOST
SO, LET ME HOLD YOU CLOSE AND NEVER FEAR
FOR I'LL ALWAYS BE BESIDE YOU MY DEAR
TENDERLY AND AFFECTIONATELY NEAR
WE'LL MAKE LOVE ALL THROUGH THE NIGHT
IN THE DARK UNTIL SUNLIGHT
AS WE LAY, LETS HOLD UP EACH OTHER IN PRAYER
YOU'RE NOTHING MORE THAN ANYONE COULD ASK FOR
MY ANSWER CAN JUST IN TIME
NOT REAL FAST, IN ORDER FOR US TO LAST
FORGETTIN OUR PAST
YOU'RE ALL I NEED
A VERY FRIEND INDEED
NEVER NEW LOVE UNTIL YOU CAME
HOPIN YOU'LL FEEL THE SAME
WE VAN GET OUT OF THIS SILLY GAME
BEING A TARGET FOR EVERYONE TO AIM
RIGHT NOW, I AM SAYIN SO LONG TO LONELINESS
AND
ON TO MY NEW SONG
OF NOT FEELIN BAD OR LOOKIN SAD
AGAIN ALL SMILES AND REAL GLAD
WITH ME YOU'LL STAY TO THIS VERY DAY
YOU'RE EVERYTHING IN A MAN'S HOPES

YOU'LL BE FOREVER LOVING ME

@ETHEKLMARGARETPOLK

YOU'RE SWEETER THAN A CANDY BAR
I'D TRAVEL NO MATTER HOW FAR
SO FAST IT WILL MAKE YOU SHIVER
LET ME PROVE MY LOVE WITH SWEET ROMANCE
ANYWAY I CAN TO GET A CHANCE
WITH A STRANGER YOU COULD BE LOST AND IN DANGER
OR LYING ON THE GROUND NEAR A FOREST RANGER
WITH A TRAGEDY THAT SHOULD NOT HAVE BEEN
BY GOING WITH ME THROUGH THE THICK AND THIN
LOVE, I'LL BRING YOU ANYTHING
JUST MAYBE A DIAMOND RING
I CAN BE YOUR HERO GUY NOT EVEN ASKING WHY
FOR YOUR SWEETNESS, I'LL GO ANYWHERE
FIGHTIN ALL YOUR NIGHTMARES
WHAT'S YOUR NAME!
HEY! I'M REAL IMPRESSED
WHAT WILL IT TAKE FOR OUR LIFE NOT TO BE A MISTAKE?
SO, YOU'LL BE FOREVER LOVING ME

I'M SORRY I MADE YOU BLUE

@ETHELMARGARETPOLK

IT'S HARD TO FINE SOMEONE THAT
MAKES YOU FEEL LIFE IS FOR REAL
A WEAVE! WIG! OR SO FINE USUALLY KEEP
YOU IN DEBT LATER ON TO REGRET
EXCITED NOW, I CAN FINALLY MEET YOU
FOR IT'LL BE SUCH A TREAT
KNOWING FROM THE BEGINNING YOUR LOVE IS TRUE
BABY, I'M SORRY I MADE YOU BLUE
BY TURNING MY HEAD AND LAYING WITH OTHERS IN BED
LATER TO FIND OUT THEY WERE OUT IN
LEFT FIELD LOOKING FOR ANY DEAL
NO MORE PLAYING GAMES!
JUST MAKING YOUR LIFE SO HAPPY AND GAY
ENOUGH OF THIS HIDE AND SEEK
ABOUT TIME NOW FOR US TO MEET
BABY, I'M SORRY I MADE YOU BLUE

GET YOUR BAGS PACKED

@ethelmargaret

BEFORE YOU WALK OUT THE DOOR, LET ME SERVE YOU NOTICE, I AM QUITE AWARE
SO, WIPE THAT UGLY LOOK OFF YOUR FACE AND STOP THE STARE
BABY! PLEASE! I REALLY DO DARE!
EACH AND EVERY DETAIL, THIS I KNOW
YOU GOTTA FIND SOME OTHER PLACE TO GO
DON'T EXPECT FROM YOUR LAWYER ANY DOUGH
YEAH! I'M GONG BACK TO BEG IF I HAVE TO AND GET IN WITH THE ONE THAT I SHOULDA DEPENDED
IN KEEPING THINGS WELL BLENDED
WHAT PEOPLE THIN CAN KISS MY ASS
MOVE OUT THE WAY SO I CAN PASS GAS
TO THE LIMITS, THIS YOU'VE DONE WITHOUT ME HAVIN ANY FUN
OUT NIGHT AFTER NIGHT! TAKIN YA COLOR AND YOU KNOW THE REST BEING AN INCREDIBLE PEST
LEAVE ME ALONE SO I CAN CONFESS
SO MANY THINGS YOU LACKED AND I COULDN'T COVER UP THE SLACK
THAT'S WHY I'M ASKIN YOU IN KINDNESS TO GET YOUR BAGS PACKED
I FOUND OUT THE TRUE MEANIN OF LOVE WHEN MY GIRL WENT INTO BRING BACK GOD'S DOVE ALL THE WAY FROM ABOVE
GET YOU BAGS PACKED! I DO NOT WANT TO HEAR ANYMORE SMACK!
JUST GET YOUR BAGS PACKED!
GET YOUR BAGS PACKED!

A HERO COMES FROM WITHIN

@ethelmargaret

TRAININ UP A CHILD WOULDN'T BE
DIFFICULT IF YOU'D STOP
LOOK AND LISTEN TO THE INSPIRED
WORD WRITTEN BY GOD
IT'S UP TO YOU ABOUT DIRECT AND ON ONE ACCORD
THIS SHOULDN'T BECOME SO HARD
EVERYONE'S LIFE IS DIFFERENT
SO DON'T LOOK AT THAT
MANY WILL PUT ON A GREAT BIG UNUSUAL
ACT WITHOUT TRUE FACTS
A HERO COMES FROM WITHIN BUT WILL LAST TO THE END
GREAT IS THY FAITHFULNESS STANDIN THROUGH
DISTRESS AND PASSIN EACH AND EVERY TESTS
A HERO COMES FROM WITHIN BUT WILL LAST TO THE END

I'D LIKE TO BE YOUR SUGAR DADDY

@ETHELMARGARETHILL

I'D LIKE TO BE YOUR SUGAR DADDY
KNOW YA WILL MAKE ME REAL HAPPY
YOUR STYLE, BABY, TURNS ME ON AND AWAY WITH MY PAIN
TOWARD MORE TO GAIN
LOOKING AT THE SUN SHINE THROUGH
YOUR FACE AFTER THE RAIN
CAN YOU FEEL MY MAGIC CLOSING UP ALL YOUR TRAGICS?
BUILDING UP TRUST IN ME IS A MUST
AND
LETS JUST GO HEAD AND FUSS GETTING
THAT OUT OF THE WAY
BECAUSE THIS IS TURNING OUT TO BE A VERY GOOD DAY
START THINKIN OF ME AS YOUR DADDY TO
START CLEANIN OUT YOUR MIND
KNOWIN IT WOULD BE JUST A MATTER OF TIME
IT'S MY DUTY CAUSE YOU'RE A REAL CUTIE
NO MOE KNOCKIN COLD YOUR PLANS
GET READY FOR THAT HOUSE AND ALL THAT LAND
GLADNESS WILL REMOVE YOUR SADNESS
I'M THE ONE YOU BLESSED AND RELIEVED MY STRESS
NOW! MY PAIN IS GONE AND I STAND STRONG THROUGH
ALL THOSES BLOWS AND ONTO JAIL THEY GO!
I'D LIKE TO BE YOUR SUGAR DADDY, YES SIR!
YES MAM! I'D LIKE TO BE YOUR SUGAR DADDY!
STRAIGHT UP! I'LL BE GOOD!

I'D LIKE TO BE YOUR SUGAR DADDY(PART2)

@ethelmargaret

Straight up I'll be good letting everyone know in the hood
Fill the house up with kids cause they kept tryin to keep you hid
See that you'll stay committed
Watch out nigga! You're bout to get hit! Please believe I surely will not miss
All upside ya head for tryin to get in my bed and swayin her to get misled
Don't ya see the signs that girls' all mine?
you got my heart and I'm keepin her away from fear now that my girls' near
Clearin all issues and throwin away her tissues
Up to the highest level leavin them who thought they were so cleaver!
Forget it niggas! Never! Ever! Never!
Down under the sheets, between ya legs, I'll eat every time we meet
Reachin out my hand hopin you'll accept
Seein that all promises will be kept
First time this way I've felt
My heart melts and a calm peace of ease
You're the essence of my very presence!
Lay back and roll up a blunt
No longer baby will you have to hunt
I'd like to be your sugar daddy!
Oh yes I do!
I'd like to be your sugar daddy!

IF YOU'LL BECOME JUST ALL MINE

@ethelmargaret

IF YOU'LL LOVE ME AS MUCH AS I DO YOU
I'LL LIGHT YOUR FIRE AND BECOME ALL OUR LIFE'S DESIRE
SO LONG HAVE I BEEN ONE OF YOUR ADMIRERS
GIRL, APPRECIATION CAN GET ME INSPIRED
AND MEET ALL YOUR COMMANDS
UP MOST, SET THE WORLD AT YOUR DEMAND
I ONCE WAS A NOBODY UNTIL YOU CAME AND MADE ME
SPECIAL
GLAD YOU SAW MY NEED AND WE BECAME TRUE FRIENDS
INDEED
IN YOU, I FOUND LIFE AND JOY
READY TO GO SAILIN! SHIP AHOY!
PLENTY OF LOVIN' HUGGIN' AND KISSIN'
ALL THE THINGS YOU'VE BEEN MISSIN'
IF YOU'LL BECOME JUST ALL MINE!

I'M GONNA FEEL YOU UP WITH TREATS

@ethehnargaret

I've heard people talk about goin out with a blast
Somehow I didn't understand until experience and havin a ball
You've been different from anyone that I've met leavin me with no regrets
I say halleluiah! When our eyes meet
No one have ever been so sweet
For the rest of our life, I'm gonna feel you up with treats
Never a last mile or steepin on up this hill
Shall I climb to make you officially mine?
I'm gonna feel you up with treats

I'M THE ONE THAT'S IN A WORLD OF TROUBLE

@ethelmargaret

Finally I can tell the truth
No longer am I concerned nor want to learn about
Who you serve so I'll move around and get just what I
Deserve plus stop getting on your nerves
Alive is somebody somewhere close to you after all
That I've put you through
Yet you come up singin and happy as can be without
No front teeth
I'm the one that's in a world of trouble
Out into no man's island will I succumb after being
So completely dumb!
I'm the one that's in a world of trouble

IT'S GOT TO BE REAL LOVE

@ethelmargaret

If you should fall
I'll be there before and after all
Honesty is needed to understand
And
Keep away from the world's demands
It's hard to have a love so real
Because
Of the way I feel
I'm real excited
Is it a crime?
Just about to lose my mind
Not asking for too much
Baby! I must have your tender touch
Let's make today and begin
Never letting tomorrow ever end
Some things can rise above
But
Never from your real true love
I'll always be your friend
Right down to the bitter end
You're just special in my heart
And
We'll never part
Thank God for a second chance
At good and true romance
I can be who I am
Because
You do care
It's got to be real love

64

JUST HERE ON THIS PLANET EARTH

@ethel

It's not just today but Christmas is all throughout the year
We should learn to spread and enjoy good cheers
Keeping that Christ like spirit of comfort to all everyday
With love and kindness
Be it is free
Just only to you and me
Someone! Somewhere! Is alone
Wondering whether they will be the next one to go
Needing words of wisdom
Baby, you better start taking it slow
Because
There is no other place to go
Just here on this planet earth
Learning to understand
Just here on this planet earth
Learning to understand
Christ's divine will
Just here on this planet earth
Learning to understand
Christ's divine will
Just here on this planet earth!

I WANT YOU REAL BAD

@ethelmargaret

If you can deny what you feel inside, then I'll
just step aside and go get in my ride
Why would you let your heart bleed when I'm the one you need-
baby, open up and receive everything that you need
I want you baby! Baby! Baby! My baby! Real bad!
Don't sit there lookin sad when I got what will make you glad
In my mind, I see the spot that makes you hot-so come
on and let's rock! Every day in front of my door!
I promise you'll rock or consider the bunny hop!
I can make you toss and turn for my good lovin baby! You'll burn
Throw away your computer-dig in deep to my rotary rooter
Again you want desire nobody else-I'll have you all to myself
Baby! Baby! Baby!
I want you really bad-real bad
I want you real bad!

KEEPIN THE HEADACHES AWAY WONDERIN WHY

AS YOU OFTEN KISSED ME BETWEEN THE LEGS
MY WORLD WRAPPED UP IN YOU NOT KNOWIN SOONER OR
LATER WE'D BE THROUGH
NOW WE'RE FIGHTIN AND ALL THE EXCITEMENT IS GONE
YOU'RE GETTING READY TO LEAVE ME ALONE
I USE TO UNDERSTAND AND HONOR YOUR EACH AND EVERY
COMMAND BUT THE DOOR SHUTS WITH YOU TELLIN ME TO
BECOME GAY
BABY, THERE IS NO OTHER WAY
I'M BALLIN NOW WITH MY GIRL NOW WHO TOOK YOU FOR A
SWIRL
I DON'T WANNA COME DOWN BECAUSE YOU'LL NEVER BE
AROUND BUT BETTER BREAK AS
LOVERS IN ORDER NOT TO BE
ENEMIES LOSIN ALL THE PRIDE AS WE ONCE WALKED IN
STRIDE
I'M SETTIN YOU FREE
BETTER FRIENDS THAN LOVERS
AS WE GO OUR SEPARATE WAYS ON AND ON TO BETTER DAYS
I'M NOT MAD SO SOMEONE ELSE IN
YOUR BOOK WILL PICK UP
YOUR LOOKS AND MAYBE THEN
YOU'LL BE FOREVER HOOKED
NEITHER OF US WANTED EACH OTHER
JUST SOMETHING TO GET BY
KEEPIN THE HEADACHES AWAY WONDERIN WHY

@em

LOSIN ALL MYSELF CONTROL

@ETHELMARGARET

THREADS THAT WEAVE TOGETHER IN A TAPESTRY
OF LIFE MEANT TO LAST FOREVER
I PROMISE YOU FOREVER
I LOOK UP AT THE MOON ABOVE MY DARKENED ROOM
SILENCE ALL MOST HURTS
THOUGH MY WORDS ARE WELL SPOKEN-I'M
NOT GONNA BE YOUR WORLD'S TOKEN
CAN'T SEEM TO FIND THE TIME OR THE WILL TO WALK AWAY
I WISHED THAT I WAS STRONG ENOUGH TO SAY GOODBYE
I KNOW IT'S OVER FOR ME BABY
THERE'S NO EASY WAY TO START SAYING THE
WORDS THAT WILL BREAK YOUR HEART
IT TEARS ME UP TO SEE YOU DIE NOT
REALLY KNOWING WHY
HEAVEN ONLY KNOWS HOW PEOPLE WHO ONCE WERE
SO CLOSE ARE NOW WALKING AROUND LIKE GHOSTS
LOSIN ALL MYSELF CONTROL

LET'S JUST LET IT BE, BABY

@ETHELMARGARET

SO GLAD YOU LET ME HOLD ON
I WAS JUST ABOUT GONE WITH NO PLACE TO STAY
LOST WITHOUT A WAY
FOREVER DOWNWARD
QUICK! SWIFT! AND FAST!
ALMOST TO THE LAST!
THEN I HEARD YOUR SOFT VOICE LET OUT A LOUD SCREAM
FIRST! I THOUGHT IT WAS SOME KIND OF DREAM
HELP ME! I DON'T KNOW WHAT TO DO
MY LIFE IS JUST ABOUT THROUGH
SLOWLY, I CAME TO A HALT REALIZING
IT WAS MY OWN FAULT
OF
NOT GETTING UP AND RUNNIN BACK INTO
YOUR ARMS CEASIN ALL THE ALARMS!
IT'S ME, LET'S JUST LET IT BE, BABY
MY HEAVEN IS JUST ABOUT TO LEAVE IF I DO NOT GO BACK
AND KEEP CLINGING ONTO YOUR HANDS
PLEASE TAKE THIS DIAMOND RING
MEMORIES OF OUR TURNABOUTS AND FLINGS
IT'S ME, BABY!
LET'S JUST LET IT BE!

LETTIN YOU GO IS A NO

@ethelmargaret

Seldomly you find a person that knows and understands the
meaning of love without any problems and able to solve
I'm highly impressed that you want to get involved
Happy now I am and no complaints
Thankin god that you let down your restraints
My friends have become few-seein that they're jealous
because you're new
Your understandin with patience is essential
Letting you go is a no
Hold on to me with both hands
I want to go up with you around your special place that
teaches about God's amazin grace
It was just a matter of time but I stood still not knowin I was
obeyin God's will until the dust cleared from all the ain'ts
You can now show me how to become a saint
Lettin you go is a no

MY FATHER'S CHILD THIS I AM

@etheimargaret

BE CAREFUL ABOUT WHAT YOU DO IN THIS LIFE
YOU STILL WILL HAVE TO ANSWER
ABOUT WHAT'S BEEN DONE
GOD'S HIGH UP ABOVE ON HIS WAY DOWN LIKE A DOVE
YOU SHOULD TRY TO CLEAN UP WHAT'S BEEN TRASHED
BECAUSE YOU ALSO MAYBE SPARED AGAIN AT THE LAST
FIRST, ADMIT YOUR QUILT ON TRYING TO SHUT HIM OUT
EVERYWHERE YOU WENT SPENDING DOWN TO THAT
EMPTY POCKET WITH NO ONE TO PAY THE RENT
I KEPT THE FAITH AND WITH PATIENCE AND STOOD ALONE
UNTIL GOD TOLD ME TO REACH OUT FOR HIS HANDS
THEN HE'S ANSWER ALL THE DEMANDS ON
THE EARTH AGAIN AT HIS COMMAND
I'M NO LONGER WEAKER OR LIFE AT A BLEAK
GOD'S TAKING ME HIGHER ON UP THE PEAK
MY FATHER'S CHILD, THIS I AM

MY LIFE'S SOFTLY IS IN YOUR SONG

@ETHEL

In your song, my life began
Write another o I can see the end
I like your style coming around every once and awhile
See you're young but not a stranger
Stop! Sitting out look like a lone ranger
My life's softly is in your song
There's such a crowd
People are kind of loud
You sing as if your know I'm longing for your love
And ready to go
Clearly and strong, I hear each word
From birth to this moment, I took a glimpse at the one
Sing my life in his song
My life's softly is in your song

MY SWEET ONE

My sweet one if you only knew what you've done
Once I was empty and lonely inside
Now you're the center of my pride
I'll always be by your side
Guess I'd never known if your other man hadn't left you alone
And you called me on the phone
Do know you're the best
Stayed away from all pests
Finally I can get some rest
My sweet one-sweetie pie
Center of my eye
My! My! Sweet one

@ethelmargaret

MYSTICAL MOMENTS LIKE THIS

@ETHELMARGARET

Mystical moment like this makes me know a real God is still in sight
Loving us yet throughout all our fight
Prophecies filled while others yet stole
Ensured the enemy to go head and take control
Do he love me? Or do he not?
This should be without a shadow of doubt
Stop thinking bad about the roots of trouble you had
Be glad for this time on happy moments you find
Open the ground for new things to be found
You'll stop on the run when you put down your guns
Pickup love, joy and peace that will give a great big release
See what you'll miss from mystical moments like this

OUR MINDS ARE REALLY ONE OF A KIND

@ethelmpolk

LOOK AROUND AND YOU'LL SEE GOD'S ANGELS WALKING AROUND EACH DAY
SOME STRAYED AWAY FROM THE TRUTH AND BEGAN TO EAT ON BABYRUTHS
    I HAVE LEARNED THAT BELIEF COMES FROM WITHIN
  AT THAT POINT WHERE YOU BEGIN
WHEN WE EXITED OUR MOM WOMB
    THERE WILL BE NO TIME TO DO A 24 HR RETURN
YOUR KNOWLEDGE ON THESE WORDS CALLED CHRISTMAS
    NOT DEPARTING BEFORE OUR CHILDREN HAVE LEARNED
AND UNDERSTAND NOW!
WE GOT TO BUILD UP THEIR MINDS BECAUSE IT REALLY IS ONE OF A KIND
IF YOU LOSE IT BY IGNORING REAL FACTS
READ AND STUDY!
GETTING YOUR APPROVAL FROM THE MOST HIGH
OUR MINDS SHOULD REALLY SEEK THE LORD FOR YOURSELF
AND SEE OUR MINDS ARE REALLY ONE OF A KIND
ONE OF A KIND
OUR MINDS ARE REALLY ONE OF A KIND!

OVER IN THE DITCH YOU WILL GO

@ethelmpolk

ENCOURAGEMENT COMES WITHOUT SETTIN A DATE NOT RATE!
GOD IS NEVER TOO LATE!
TEARS MAY SHED, AFTER ALL THAT YOU HAVE READ
YOUR HEART HURTING AND SAT MANY DAYS
WONDERING WHY DO IT HAVE BE THIS WAY?
SILENCE IS REALLY GOLDEN AS YOU CONTINUE TO GROW
OLDER WHILE DAY AND ONTO THE NIGHT
SOON, YOU WILL SEE GODS HEAVENLY LIGHT
THEN BRIGHTER! BRIGHTER1 AND YOUR BURDENS WILL
BECOME LIGHTER BECAUSE WHO THE SUN SET FREE
SHOULD BE FREE WITHOUT THE ATTENTION OF ANY HEED
CURSED IS A MAN THAT TURNS AND LOOK BACK
YOU ARE ON YOUR WAY TO A POWER OF NO LACK
TURNING YOUR CHEEKS AS YOU WERE SMACKED
YOUR ENEMIES WILL NOT BE THERE
FOR TOUCHIN GODS ANOINTED AND TRYING TO DO HARM
WILL CAUSE SUCH A GREAT ALARM
YOO LSYR1 TOO LATE! GOD SET OFF THE ALARM AND
OVER IN THE DITCH YOU WILL GO!
TOO LATE1 TOO LATE! GOD SET OFF THE ALARM AND OVER
IN THE DITCH YOU WILL GO!

PLEASE FORGIVE AND LET ME SEE YOU AGAIN

@emp

STOP SAYING YOU'RE TOO OLD
GOD KNOWS I'VE REALLY FOUND GOLD
YOU KNEW ME BEFORE I DID MYSELF
THAT'S WHY I DON'T WANT ANYONE ELSE
YOU'VE BEEN MY CONSTANT CARE
THROUGH ALL MY WHOLLY NIGHTMARES
PLEASE FORGIVE AND COME BACK ONCE AGAIN
MY BABY!
BE AGAIN ALWAYS WAITIN
AND
REMEMBERING OUR WONDERFUL TIMES
CONTINUING TO KEEP ME ON YOUR MIND
GOT SUCH A REAL DEAL IN THE MIDST OF ALL YOUR HEAT
KNOW I LEFT YOU ALL ALONE
NOT EVEN BY ANY TELEPHONES
IF IT IS ANY COMFORT OR CHEER
SOMEHOW, I STILL KNEW YOU WERE NEAR
MY MIND WAS REALLY MESHED UP AND HAD TO DRINK OF
THAT BITTER CUP!
PLEASE FORGIVE AND LET ME SEE YOU AGAIN!

QUICKLY! LET'S START NEW

@ethel

<u>DON'T ASK ME ANY QUESTIONS BUT I'M HERE NOW</u>
<u>IF YOU MUST KNOW, I'M GETTING READY FOR US TO GO</u>
Let's take out a little time and party-hittin the bars-jammin with the dj
Throwin him over and over some extra pay-it had to be this way
What else can I say?-the only direction to get you paid
Your time is over due
Quickly! Let's start new
Listen to the beat so we can get up on the dance floor
Steppin with each beat as we meet and greet
Times were hard but it's worth all as you get your max
pay right down the line from town to town
Quickly! Let's start new

QUIT YA STRESSIN AND START IMPRESSIN

@ethelmargaret

My protection, light, joy and sorrow are just a few from above that
will comfort and strengthen our life through pain, misery and strife
To you I must tell wherever I go don't stop even though you may have to hop
The enemy will never stop until he gets your soul
That's his main goal
I don't know about you but mine he ain't gonna get
because God's not through blessin me yet
That's a sure bet
Quit ya stressin and start impressin

YOU GOTTA GO HEAD AND PAY THE COST

@ethelmargaret

So I chose a different path which led to death of my mind
Somehow I thought things would work out just fine
And they'd become all mine but I neglected to see
That shined face was for real paid by testifyin of god's divine will
with my bags and shoes in my hand onto other doors undetermined
but out of the way because together we'll not miss a single flight
I just got to see in reality I was sick because this Jesus had
me locked for the last count not losin any amounts
Lookin around but nobody was there askin myself
what is this a horrible nightmare
No one would hear my pleads down on bendin knees
beggin for someone to hold on to me before I get lost
Laughin sayin sister you gotta go head and pay the cost
So sorry my sister but you gotta go head and pay the cost
You gotta go head and pay the cost

YOU SHOWED WISDOM THROUGH YOUR FAITH

@ethelmargaret

*Hard times continued to block our way but I waited with patience in
the mist of trouble because I believe you'd get to me on the double
Spinnin, turnin and tumbling suppressed down by angry crowds yelling
and screamin, burnin with their lusts makin up all sorts of fuss
Yet I just would not cuss because you're showin wisdom
through faith that I was makin a big mistake
Within your heart, you raptured up my words and held on with the
holy spirit not seein but after that audible voice you did complete
You showed wisdom through your faith*

YOUR HEART BELONGS TO SOMEONE ELSE

@ETHELMARGARET

YOU SAID IT WAS BEST TO FORGET ABOUT NOT
HOLDIN OUT THROUGH THE TEST-I CAN'T GIVE IT A
REST ABOUT THE MEMORIES THAT WE SHARED
THOUGH I'LL STILL SING HAPPY SONGS
OF HOW WE BELONGED
IN THE QUICKNESS OF THE NIGHT-OUR LIVES
WENT OUT OF SIGHT-TOO LATE TOO MUSCLE UP
A FIGHT BECAUSE YOU WERE TRULY RIGHT
YOUR HEART BELONGS TO SOMEONE ELSE
ALL OF WHAT MIGHT HAVE BEEN
WILL BE LEFT UNANSWERED
BUT
YOU MUST KNOW BEFORE YOU GO- YOUR LOVE
SURELY CAME STRAIGHT FROM ABOVE
THIS I OVERLOOKED AND WILL NOT GET AGAIN
YOUR HEART BELONGS TO SOMEONE ELSE

YOUR LOVE WILL ALWAYS BE
UNITED AND ALSO INVITED

@ethelmargaret

A kiss is every indication that your heart is right and
endless possibilities won't keep me out of your sight
Stars will shine cause you're a true love of mine
In the morning, we'll still be together
At any type of weather
Let's take a slow and easy ride
Tell me you'll always stay by my side
A night like this may never come again
Keep in touch and always be my friend
The time is now and you're a star
No matter how far
Pick love up and pass it on
In a short time, we'll be strong
Coming together not divided
You'll be well provided
Do not sing a sad song
For I won't be gone long
Your love will always be united

YOU'VE BEEN JUST THAT GOOD TO ME

@ethel Margaret

I'm still going to place everything at your feet for you kept things real neat
With your love by my side, keeps me up with great pride
As I walk in stride you are my queen because I'm now a king
Plenty of wealth to unfold
Just been waitin to be told
You've been just that good to me
Your days will be sunny and blue cause you've been just that true
As we make love, I feel warm sensations
Baby stay my inspiration
Keep lyin in my arms
So I can make things at ease
You've been just that good to me

SOON YOU'LL BE TOP NOTCH

@ETHELMARGARET

A REAL FRIEND WILL STICK WITH YOU UNTIL
THE END DURING WHATEVER TO AMEND
WHERE THE HURT BEGIN-WORKIN IT OUT
THROUGH THE THICK AND THIN
JESUS IS THAT PERSON IN MIND KEPT SAFE AND SOUND
LOOKIN HIGH AND LOW FROM A MOUNTAIN
TOP REMOVING ALL STUMBLIN BLOCKS
SO CONTINUE ON YOUR JOURNEY AS
CHRISTIAN ON THE WATCH
SOON YOU'LL BE TOP NOTCH
BEAUTIFUL WILL YOU BE ALONG SIDE JESUS AND ME
I'M TELLIN YOU NOW AND NOT AT YOUR GRAVE SITE
BECAUSE
I LOVE YOU NOW WITH ALL MY MIGHT KEEPIN
AWAY FUSSIN-CUSSIN- NOR A FIGHT
I'M WANTIN YOU ALWAYS TO LIVE-CONTINUE
ON WITH THE BEAUTY YOU GIVE
SO AGAIN, ONWARD YOUR JOURNEY
AS A CHRISTIAN WATCHIN
SOON! YOU'LL BE TOP NOTCH

SOMEONE WRONGLY MISREAD

@emargaret

If only I'd known before taking others command that Jesus is
real and I couldn't stop you from makin deals plus no longer
a big wheel with your enemy seal stamped in your head
Nothing else now but go back to bed someone wrongly misread
because you're one of God's people who couldn't be misled
Shoulda stopped and listened when my childhood reflected there is no one to
depend on but that mighty one up in the sky instead of eatin that fool's pie
Goin down slow without much life thinkin someone would take
me up in their body to that heavenly place but now I see it's
all about me following divine directions that I didn't do
So I'll go head and pay the price in takin
another's advice without thinkin twice
Someone wrongly misread because God's people can't be misled

STILL MIXING IT

@ETHELMARGARET

TELL ME WHAT TO DO
DON'T SAY WE'RE THROUGH
PROMISES SOME ARE BROKEN
LET'S GET THAT OUT IN THE OPEN
LIFE IS AT HAND
I'M EVEN AT YOUR COMMAND
GRASS IS GREENER ON THE OTHER SIDE
I CAME BACK TO TAKE YOU UP IN MY RIDE
A 2000 YEAR FANTASY
GOD IS MY STRENGTH
TAKE ME TO ANY LENGTH
SO GET OUT OF MY FACE
TAKE ANOTHER SPACE
WHEN YOU SEE THE ENEMY AT HAND
ON SUCK A HIGH GREAT DEMAND
JESUS IS LORD
EVERYTHING ON ONE ACCORD
THAT'S WHEN YOU KNOW
LIFE IS AT ITS BEST
STILL MIXING IT

STRAIGHT FROM MY HEART, I WILL

@ethel Margaret

In my wildest dreams, you came to me just like ice cream
Taste so real with each of my fingers a feel
My life have changed in the midst of every rearrange
Lookin at you by my side makes me feel real proud
So! So! Strong to tell that dope man so long!
Thanks to you I will get better as the sun rises
I want to live forever
Straight from my heart, I will
No matter what the storm-I will not become alarmed
Then only and only you will I protect from all harm
You came alone just in the nick of time
Thought that I'd end of losin my mind
I want to live forever
Straight from my heart, I will

SHUT THE DOOR AND GET OUT OF MY LIFE

@ethel

You may as well remove your head off of the pillows on my bed
For our love is truly dead
At day light, let's promise not to fight
It's no use and I haven't an excuse
Guess it wasn't love-so let's just say goodbye
Stop all the wondering why
Because we gave it a good try
Stop looking hopeless cause I'm no fool
I been to plenty of schools in knowing there are no such rules but you
didn't give a damn runnin around with any man named sam
I tried to close my eyes and play blind but I
couldn't for you were suppose to be mine
Time and time, I asked for a touch because I love you so very much
Take your things and give me back my diamond ring-
shut the door and get out of my life

SURELY BABY GIRL I'LL BE THERE

@emargaret

I don't know when the tears stopped but I heard a audible
voice saying let your child make her choice
As I looked up to see her face with a smile sayin
baby you can still have your space
No more pity or full of groans because you're an adult now
Ready to leave home but remember if times ever get to hard and
your burdens not able to bear close your eyes and call out for me
Surely I'll be there
Betta! Baby girl I'll be there

THANK YOU ONCE AGAIN, PLEASE

@ethelmargaret

Every day I say a prayer for you to please stay on my mind while
the enemies out shootin us down any where we can be found
Let me become close and focus on what you need
the most other than the holyghost
Thank you for being near and keepin me away from any fear
Nothing but good cheers allowing room for improvement
A spirit forgivin will make life worth the livin
Amen! Amen! Amen!
Every now and then you're the one to defend
My only depend
A wonderful little angel wrapped in a dirty blanket sent to this world with
wisdom as a guide to savin all sinners that desire so they can become winners
Thank you once again, please
On our grounds did he walk around and talk
receiving all that wanted unto him
Thank you once again, please (2)

THOSE OTHER FELLOWS HAD TO BE OUT OF THEIR MIND!

@ethelmpolk

NOTHIN COULD EVER BECOME BETTER
WITH YOU IN MY SIGHTS
TROUBLED AND BURDENED DOWN
BUT AS I LOOK UP AT YOUR
FACE THAT SHINE
THOSE OTHER FELLOWS HAD TO BE OUT OF THEIR MIND
CLIMAX CHANGES
SO! LIFE'S NEVER THE SAME
EACH DAY IS NEW FULL OF SOMETHINGS
YOU'VE NEVER BEEN
THROUGH
YET! YOU HELD ON STRAIGHT AND
WALKED TALL AMONG IT ALL
THOSE OTHER FELLOWS BABY HAD
TO BE OUT OF THEIR MIND
YOU'RE SO FINE! SO FINE AND ALL MINE!
THOSE OTHER FELLOWS HAD TO BE OUT OF THEIR MIND!

THINGS AIN'T GONNA WORK OUT FINE

@ethelmargaret

YOU MAYBE THINKIN ABOUT GOING OUT THERE TRICKIN
AND TAKIN ALL THE WORLD'S LICKIN
LET'S WORK ON THIS
SO YOU CAN NOT MISS
THEY TOLD ME NOT TO STICK AROUND
CAUSE YOU WON'T BE FOUND
TO THINK I WAS TRIPPIN! STRESSIN!
ALMOST THINKIN BOUT STOP DICKIN!
WHILE YOU WERE INVESTIN AND YOUR
LIFE NOT ANYMORE MESSIN
I DESERVED OVERTIME FOR THINGS DID WORK OUT FINE
I SENSE IT WHEN WE'RE CLOSE THAT I'M
NOT THE ONE YOU LOVE THE MOST
BECAUSE YOU CAN'T GET MY SOUL AND MOVE
ME ROUND LIKE REMOTE CONTROL
BABY! HONEY PLEASE!
THINGS AIN'T GONNA WORK OUT FINE
A NIGGA LIKE YOU AIN'T HARD TO FIND
THINGS AIN'T GONNA WORK OUT FINE

TOGETHER BABY I MUST INSIST

@ETHELMARGARET

I FINALLY FOUND THAT SPECIAL FEELING
WHICH I'VE BEEN LOOKIN FOR
TO! HERE! AND FAR! MY MIND'S NOW AT EASE
YOU'RE THE ONE I WANT TO PLEASE
NO LONGER WILL I LET THEM TEASE
STRONG FLAMES OF FIRE ARE YET BURNING
MY BODIES STILL YEARNING
INSIDE YOU FILL ME WITH PRIDE
SET MY FEET WALKING WITH STRIDE
NO LONGER WILL I RESIST-TOGETHER BABY I MUST INSIST
YOUR LOVE ONLY, I'M HOLD ON
ANY OTHERS MIGHT AS WELL GET GONE
I APOLOGIZE FOR ALL THE WRONG DONE
NO LONGER WILL I RESIST-TOGETHER BABY I MUST INSIST
TOGETHER BABY I MUST INSIST

USE THE WISDOM AND KNOWLEDGE
THAT YOU'VE ACQUIRED

@emargaret

Some may think its easy lookin people while performin
But many faces can become very alarmin
Smile with knives covered in arm pits waitin to make that big hit
Throw me over in a ditch cutting out my each and every pitch
Sayin they ya brother or sister too stealin and takin everything from you
Even got the nerve trying a curve and jumpin in my shoes not
rememberin there've the one that will lose and be left standin
There accused
Free as it may seem but this is not true
So many changes not to rearrange keepin away from that type of game
Refusing even to give them your name
Use the wisdom and knowledge that you've acquired

UNTIL

@EMP

Only until one learn to love each other
Only until we stop killing one another
Selling drugs and using them in our arms
Caused many decisions made on alarm
Until then you'll know what it is to be free
Appreciate life now and who make the sacrifices anyhow
Love is the essence of our very presence
So, let's not take things for granted
While still here on this planet
Then finally ourselves and everyone else will know what it is to be free!

WANTED AND NEEDED -WAITIN JUST FOR YOU

@ETHELMARGARET

Love becomes nice after you pay the price
Finally found a love so true
not even over due
you're all I want and need
time for the world to take heed
glad you're my queen
meeting every one of my dreams
that special way you touch my heart
makes me not want to stay apart
now I'm believing happiness is mine
came just right in time
so nice and right
I know we'll never ever fight
For I'll always love you with all my might
So, I'm just going to hold on real tight
Thanks for caring and being around
Open the door to my heart and guess what I found
Wanted and needed
Waiting just for you

WE'RE TOGETHER NOW

@ETHELMARGARET
NOTHING ELSE MATTERS-COME RAIN OR SHINE
I'M SO GLAD TO KNOW THAT YOU'RE REALLY MINE
ITS OVERDUE AFTER ALL THE CHANGES
YOU'VE BEEN PUT THROUGH
BUT
OUR LIFE WILL WORK OUT FINE
JUST IN THE NICK OF TIME
EVERYDAY LET'S MAE IT LAST-
FORGETTING ABOUT THE PAST
I MADE MISTAKES AND SO DID YOU
SOMEHOW
WE STARTED TOGETHER STUCK LIKE GLUE
ON THE WAY TO HAPPINESS AGAIN BRAND NEW
WE'RE TOGETHER NOW

WHO YOU WERE FROM THE BEGININ
IS THAT PATHWAY YOU SHOULD HAVE
TAKEN WITHOUT A SECOND LOOK

@ethel

*Standin up is just that-a statement of truth
and reality that's from the beginin
As you came out of your mothers' womb in assistin you not to become doomed
Hold on to what you believe even though you may not be relieved
At the very moment that you stopped-is when Jesus was about to amend
but you turned your back and on another shoulder thinkin they'd depend
All your fame and fortune is now gone cause you wouldn't handle your
fear and kept makin excuses why you didn't or ran and hid from stardom
Who you were from the beginin is that pathway you
should have taken without a second look*

WHATEVER YOU WANT ME TO DO

@ethelmargaret

Now is the time we can be alone
No friends or the telephone
We've always been on the go
Findin little for us to do
I need to feel your sweet love
Expressed to me directly from above
Let's share a lot of pleasure far high and above measures
We've become a great pair

Thanks by all means of your time to share the way our bodies feel inside
Bubbling out with great pride
Leaning on God as our guide
Wonderful and marvelous life will be
Long as I have you here with me, every part of me by chance
Forever in sweet romance
Let me take my time and love you from head to toes
Gentleness fully completed
As you lay by my side
Whatever you want me to do

WHEN I LOOK INTO YOUR EYES

@ethel

WHEN I LOOKED INTO YOUR EYES
IT CAUGHT ME BY A TOTAL SURPRISE
SUCH A COMFORT OF LOVE
HIGH FROM ABOVE
SADNESS DISAPPEARED
MY MIND WAS CLEARED
JUST TO HAVE YOU NEAR
WHEN I LOOK INTO YOUR EYES
AS I SIT BESIDE MOM AND DAD
REMEMBER ALL THE THINGS THAT WE HAD
LIFE IS NOW NOT SO BAD
NO MORE AM I SAD
THOUGH MY FAMILIES LOVE IS A GODLY GIFT
EACH MORNIN AS I RISE IT GIVES ME A TOTAL LIFT
YOU GAVE ME THE CHANCE FOR SWEET ROMANCE
EXCITED THAT I STOPPED AND TOOK A GLANCE
LET ME SING YOU A SONG NOT SO LONG
BECAUSE MY LONELY MOMENTS ARE ALL GONE
WHEN I LOOK INTO YOUR EYES
SEEING THAT WE'LL NOT DISAGREE
FOR OUR MIND INPUTS YOU AND ME
I DON'T WANT TO HEAR WHAT'S SAID OUTSIDE
CAUSE YOU STAYED BY MY SIDE
WHEN I LOOK INTO YOUR EYES

WITH THIS RING

@ethel

Just in this little time, you've become heavily on my mind
Is this real or am I in a dream seein you smiling
and lickin down in my between?
Let the others be foolish cause I won't complain
There're the ones left lame from playing stupid games
On my knees I'll go, thankin the man above who sent you flyin
When your life became thin not knowin where
to begin, here I am with this ring
I'm askin makin it perfectly clear, I always want you near with this ring
Baby! Baby! With this ring

WHATEVER YOU SO DESIRE

@ETHELMARGARET

BORN AND RAISED IN A SLUM TYPE CITY
THAT'S WHY I SEEM SO WITTY
NOWHERE TO PACK IN THAT ONE ROOM SHACK
SLEPT UNTIL DAWN-WENT OUT LOOKING FOR PAWN
NOTHING TO EAT-WENT OUT TO THE BEAT
MY FATHER DIDN'T WORK-SUCH A BIG JERK
MOM TOOK ALL THE LICK-TOLD ME NOT TO KICK
STOP LETTING LIFE PASS YOU BY
LATER ON, YOU'LL WONDER WHY
SOMEONE WILL TURN YOUR SKIES BLUE AND BE REAL TRUE
IN MY MIND IS A CASTLE BUILT FROM SAND
JUST BY A SINGLE ONE HAND
GOT SO MUCH MONEY-IT'S ALL YOURS HONEY
IF ANYONE'S AT YOUR AGE- JUST GIVE ME A PAGE
WHATEVER YOU SO DESIRE

I'M SORRY I MADE YOU BLUE

@ETHELMARGARETPOLK

*IT'S HARD TO FINE SOMEONE THAT
MAKES YOU FEEL LIFE IS FOR REAL
A WEAVE! WIG! OR SO FINE USUALLY KEEP
YOU IN DEBT LATER ON TO REGRET
EXCITED NOW, I CAN FINALLY MEET YOU
FOR IT'LL BE SUCH A TREAT
KNOWING FROM THE BEGINNING YOUR LOVE IS TRUE
BABY, I'M SORRY I MADE YOU BLUE
BY TURNING MY HEAD AND LAYING WITH OTHERS IN BED
LATER TO FIND OUT THEY WERE OUT IN
LEFT FIELD LOOKING FOR ANY DEAL
NO MORE PLAYING GAMES!
JUST MAKING YOUR LIFE SO HAPPY AND GAY
ENOUGH OF THIS HIDE AND SEEK
ABOUT TIME NOW FOR US TO MEET
BABY, I'M SORRY I MADE YOU BLUE*

BRING HER BACK TO ME MINE

@ETHELMARGARETPOLK

SUCH A SHAME AND I'M THE ONE TO BLAME
OF NOT COMIN STRAIGHT TO THE POINT
IN TELLIN YOU HOW I FELT
SITTIN STILL ABOUT TO MELT WONDERIN WHY
SOMEONE WAS NOT THERE TO GIVE ME HELP
NOT A DAY GO BY THAT YOU DO NOT CROSS MY MIND
BECAUSE YOU WERE SO NICE AND KIND
WOMEN LIKE YOU ARE HARD TO FIND
I LOVE YOU OUT LOUD AND IN FRONT OF CROWDS
YES, I'VE BEEN VERY PROUD THAT
YOU WERE IN MY PRESENCE
BY TAKING UP THE SLACK REGAININ BACK
EVERYTHING THAT YOU LACKED
I MIGHT AS WELL FACE THE FACTS
THESE YOUNG GIRL'S SHOULD BE TIRED OF MY ACT
AND BEGAN GETTING THEIR BAGS PACKED
SO, I AM CLOSIN THE DOORS FOR IMPROVEMENT
THIS I'VE LEARNED TO PRAY
BRING HER BACK TO ME MINE
LORD! PLEASE BRING HER BACK TO BE MINE

YOU'LL BE FOREVER LOVING ME

@ETHEKLMARGARETPOLK

YOU'RE SWEETER THAN A CANDY BAR
I'D TRAVEL NO MATTER HOW FAR
SO FAST IT WILL MAKE YOU SHIVER
LET ME PROVE MY LOVE WITH SWEET ROMANCE
ANYWAY I CAN TO GET A CHANCE
WITH A STRANGER YOU COULD BE LOST AND IN DANGER
OR LYING ON THE GROUND NEAR A FOREST RANGER
WITH A TRAGEDY THAT SHOULD NOT HAVE BEEN
BY GOING WITH ME THROUGH THE THICK AND THIN
LOVE, I'LL BRING YOU ANYTHING
JUST MAYBE A DIAMOND RING
I CAN BE YOUR HERO GUY NOT EVEN ASKING WHY
FOR YOUR SWEETNESS, I'LL GO ANYWHERE
FIGHTIN ALL YOUR NIGHTMARES
WHAT'S YOUR NAME!
HEY! I'M REAL IMPRESSED
WHAT WILL IT TAKE FOR OUR LIFE NOT TO BE A MISTAKE?
SO, YOU'LL BE FOREVER LOVING ME

YOU'RE EVERYTHING IN A MAN'S HOPES

@ETHELMARGARETPOLK

I LOVE YOU THE MOST
SO, LET ME HOLD YOU CLOSE AND NEVER FEAR
FOR I'LL ALWAYS BE BESIDE YOU MY DEAR
TENDERLY AND AFFECTIONATELY NEAR
WE'LL MAKE LOVE ALL THROUGH THE NIGHT
IN THE DARK UNTIL SUNLIGHT
AS WE LAY, LETS HOLD UP EACH OTHER IN PRAYER
YOU'RE NOTHING MORE THAN ANYONE COULD ASK FOR
MY ANSWER CAN JUST IN TIME
NOT REAL FAST, IN ORDER FOR US TO LAST
FORGETTIN OUR PAST
YOU'RE ALL I NEED
A VERY FRIEND INDEED
NEVER NEW LOVE UNTIL YOU CAME
HOPIN YOU'LL FEEL THE SAME
WE VAN GET OUT OF THIS SILLY GAME
BEING A TARGET FOR EVERYONE TO AIM
RIGHT NOW, I AM SAYIN SO LONG TO LONELINESS
AND
ON TO MY NEW SONG
OF NOT FEELIN BAD OR LOOKIN SAD
AGAIN ALL SMILES AND REAL GLAD
WITH ME YOU'LL STAY TO THIS VERY DAY
YOU'RE EVERYTHING IN A MAN'S HOPES

Printed in the United States
By Bookmasters